Green Line 6 G9

Workbook

W0213468

von
Jon Marks
Alison Wooder
sowie
Jennifer Baer-Engel
Louise Carleton-Gertsch
Geraldine Greenhalgh
Arnd Nadolny

herausgegeben von
Harald Weisshaar

Ernst Klett Verlag
Stuttgart · Leipzig

VOCABULARY

1 Make your voice heard → SB 10/1

a) *How can people make their voices heard? Add to the mind map.*

You can make your voice heard by …

- ________________
- *joining a* ________________
- *signing a* ________________
- ________________
- ________________
- ________________
- ________________
- *writing a* ________________
- ________________

b) *For each idea in a) think of a situation in which this is a very effective way to make your voice heard. Make notes in your exercise book.*

2 Make a difference → SB 11/2

VOCABULARY

a) *Complete the dialogue between Guy and Annabel with the collocations below. Change their form if necessary.*

	+	
change | make (3x) | feel | do | get (2x) | stand | understand |	+	a difference | sb's attention | involved | a statement | up for | sb's behaviour | strongly | sb's part | the issues | a better place

Guy: Do you really think that being a political activist actually ________________?

Annabel: Of course I do, but that's not the main reason I decided to ________________ in protests and student politics. In my opinion, if you ________________ about something, you should ________________ your beliefs. You have to at least try to ________________ the world ________________.

Guy: So you're just ________________ about what you believe in?

Annabel: No, that's not what I meant. I'm ________ my ________ to make the world a little better.

Guy: Do you think dangerous stunts are the best way to ________________ people's ________________?

Annabel: It depends. It's not enough just to say there's a problem. You need to help people to ________________. Then they're more likely to ________________ their ________________.

SPEAKING MK

b) *Research a protest stunt and give a two-minute presentation on whether it was a good way to make one's voice heard.*

WRITING **3** MK

Write a quiz → SB 13/7

a) *Create a quiz with five questions about the people in power in the US and UK. Use a website, app or other tool to easily design and share your quiz. Look at the example: one answer is right, the other two are wrong.*

b) *Exchange your quiz with another group and do their quiz.*

The UK prime minister lives
a) in Buckingham Palace
b) at 10 Downing Street
c) in the White House

READING **4**

SDGs: Saving the world together → SB 13/9; S1, S2

Read the information about the UN's Sustainable Development Goals (SDGs). Are the statements true or false? Tick ✔ the correct answer and give line numbers.

In 2016 the United Nations (UN) established new goals to make the world a better place. Covering different areas of life such as education, food, health and energy use, the 17 goals were named "Sustainable Development Goals" (SDGs). The UN plans to reach them by 2030.

The SDGs have become popular and many people volunteer to help with reaching the goals. Their activism has brought about projects in many UN countries, which proves that individuals can influence the world.

One of these people is Herman van Veen from the Netherlands. He works as a musician, clown, actor and storyteller, inspiring his audience with humorous lyrics. He has been speaking out for the rights of children since 1963 and he believes the world could be more peaceful if the rights of children were respected. Four of the 17 SDGs focus on children's right to a better life, meaning: no poverty, good health and well-being, quality education and reduced inequalities.

Children make up about 20 % of the world's population and a billion of them have an uncertain future, meaning that their future health and well-being are not secured. Van Veen makes people in power and control responsible for not making children's rights a priority.

While children's rights are a big part of the SDGs, projects related to the economy are also represented. The challenge here is to reduce our economy's ecological footprint as much as possible. To set an example, French diver and film producer Jérôme Delafosse and ex-marine Victorien Erussard built a large catamaran that runs on sustainable power only. They sailed 9,000 km from Europe to the Caribbean to show how efficient wind and solar energy are. Sailing for 60 days, they produced their own drinking water and stopped in only two harbours to buy food.

Clearly, we 'as the world's population' are facing a huge task right now, but with the help of many activists, the SDGs may be achieved.

	true	false	line number(s)
1. The UN planned to reach the SDGs within 14 years.	☐	☐	
2. There are lots of SDG projects in countries outside of the UN.	☐	☐	
3. Van Veen believes that children's rights should not be part of the UN's SDGs.	☐	☐	
4. Some SDGs such as 'no poverty' and 'quality education' focus on children's rights.	☐	☐	
5. Delafosse and Erussard's catamaran used wind and solar power only to cross the Atlantic Ocean.	☐	☐	
6. The trip from Europe to the Caribbean took 90 days and covered a distance of 6,000 km.	☐	☐	
7. The crew didn't have to buy drinking water because they brought enough for the trip.	☐	☐	
8. Activists are helping to improve the world by supporting the SDGs.	☐	☐	

Unit 1 Never enough?

VOCABULARY

1 Think before you buy

→ SB 15/3; S2

a) *Find adjectives and nouns for the verbs in the grid, where possible. Use a dictionary for help.*

verb	adjective	noun
to achieve	______ (= can be achieved)	
to boycott		
to consume	______ (= can be consumed)	
to dispose of	______ (= can be disposed of)	
to exceed	______ (= too much)	
to impact		

b) *Complete what activist Hakim said in his podcast. You can use some of the verbs, adjectives and nouns in a). Change the verb form where necessary.*

"It's almost Halloween time again, and my local supermarket is *full* of Halloween stuff – toys, masks, costumes … It's all super-cheap, too. Most of it will be used once and then ______________. These low prices are only possible because Western ______________ aren't paying the environmental costs. And then there are the social costs paid by workers in developing countries. Of course, it's not just Halloween. Our ______________ consumption in general is ______________ negatively on the whole planet. It's well known that the ______________ of human activity is ______________ what the planet can support. It's time for us to put a stop to over-______________ and think twice before we buy something new. In the past, companies changed the way they do business after being ______________. So maybe we need to ______________ companies that produce under unfair conditions and don't care about the environment. If that changed the way more people thought about this issue, then it would be a real ______________ for those of us who'd like to save the planet!"

VOCABULARY

2 The life cycle of a straw hat[1] → SB 17/2b)

Underline the correct words to complete the text from an environmental organisation's website.

Let's take what seems an innocent example of cheap fashion. Most of what we call 'straw hats' are actually made of paper. Millions are sold every summer, and many are so cheap that they are considered almost **profitable / disposable / harmful**. Nevertheless, they have a significant ecological **emission / load / footprint**. First, the paper must be bleached and, in some cases, **spun / dyed / fled**, and then the **chemicals / pesticides / textiles** from that often end up **letting off / contaminating / disposing of** the local environment. Since most of them are made in Asia, they may have to be **shipped / treated / picked** a long way to their destination, causing more CO_2 **chemicals / textiles / emissions**. In addition, most of them also contain a small amount of **pollution / groundwater / fabric** so they cannot easily be **bleached / transported / recycled** and are sent to **disposal / landfill / emissions** instead. Straw hats are just a tiny part of the **global / average / raw** and extremely **organic / average / profitable** fashion industry, but they demonstrate how **harmful / profitable / contaminated** to the environment this industry can be.

LISTENING

3 Rent your clothes → SB 17/2c); S29

a) *Look at the infographic from the website of a new clothing rental[2] business. How do you think the business works? Write down 2–3 sentences in your exercise book.*

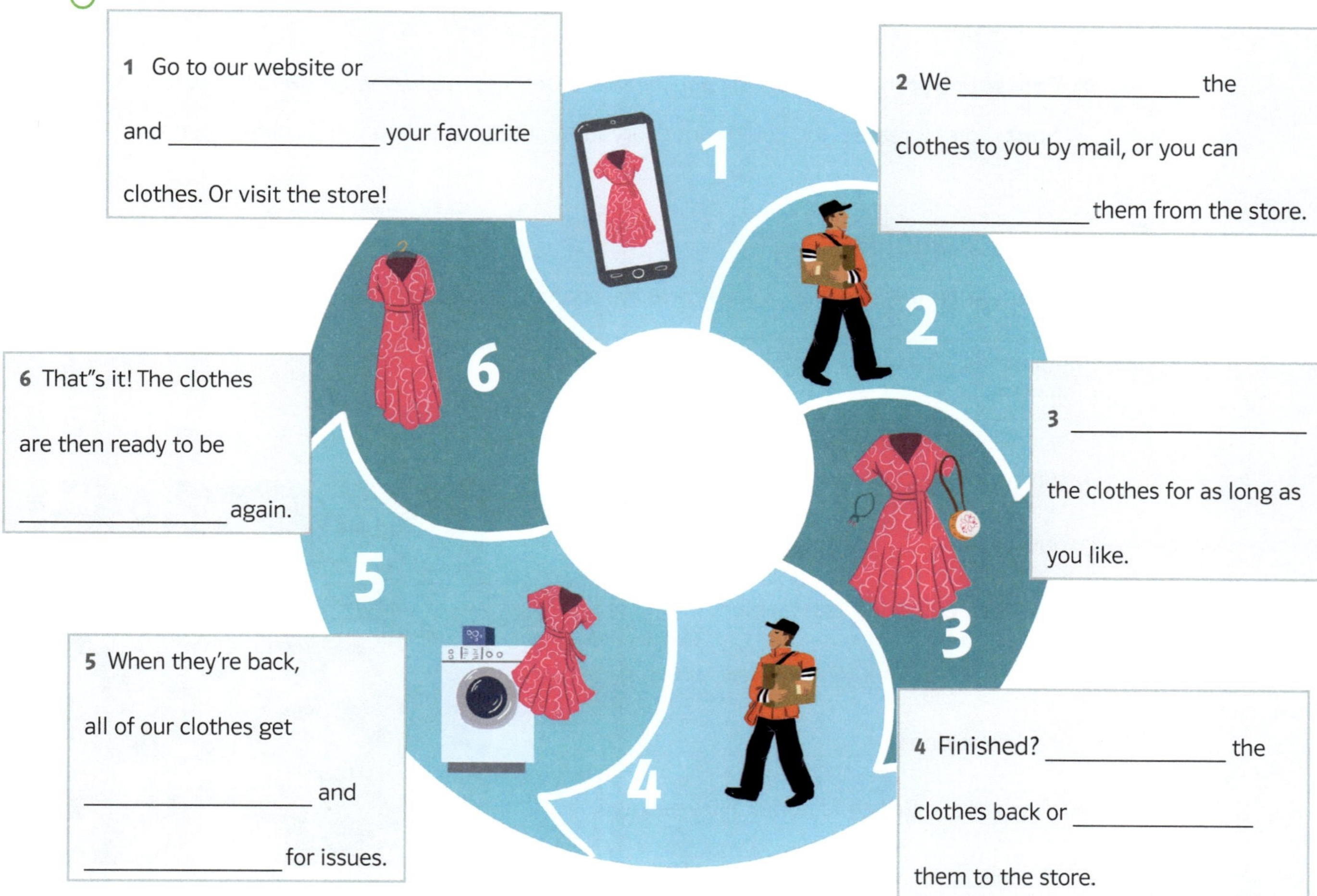

A1 b) *Listen to a radio interview with Eleanor Shannon, the owner of the business, and check if you were right. Then listen again and complete the infographic.*

c) *After the interview, the radio station posts about it on their social media. They ask if you would rent clothes instead of buying them. Write an online comment in which you explain your opinion.*

1 straw hat ['strɔː ˌhæt] hat made out of dried grass ○ **2** rental [rentl] the act of renting sth out

GRAMMAR

4 <I'm renting clothes because …> → SB 17/4; <G1>

a) *Choose all the linking words that you can use to join the two sentences together. Write them down in the grid.*

although | where | until ✔ | than | because | even though | till ✔ | since | before | as

	main clause	subordinate clause	linking word(s)
1.	I didn't realise you could rent everyday clothes.	I heard that radio interview.	*until / till / …*
2.	Renting clothes may seem more expensive.	Buying them may seem less expensive.	
3.	Renting may actually be cheaper than buying them.	You don't waste money on clothes you only wear once or twice.	
4.	I've quite often bought clothes that don't really fit me.	I tried them on in the shop.	
5.	I need to find out.	I can rent everyday clothes too.	

b) *Choose one of the linking words and join the sentences in a). Use your exercise book.*

Start: I didn't realise you could rent everyday clothes until I heard that radio interview.

GRAMMAR

5 Working conditions → SB 18/5; G2

Choose suitable linking words to complete the sentences about working conditions.

purpose: so | so that | in order to | in case
manner: like | as | as if | as though | just as

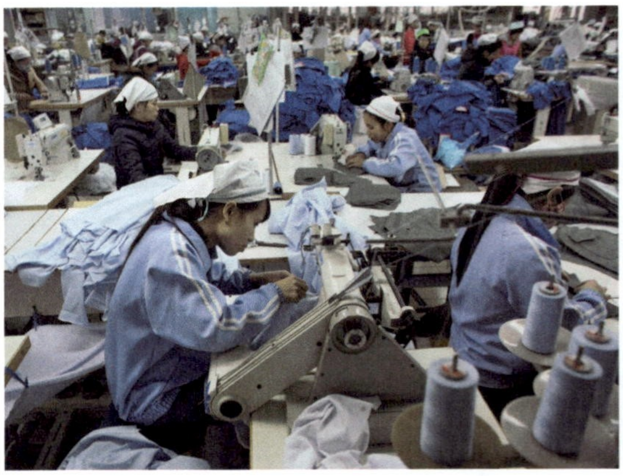

1. Around the world, people are working for very low pay ____________ we in the West can enjoy 'fast fashion'.
2. Millions of garment[1] makers are working in very bad conditions, ____________ they were in British factories 150 years ago.
3. We talk about working conditions in Victorian Britain ____________ they were a thing of the past.
4. Companies are making someone somewhere work for as little as $1 a day ____________ sell cheap T-shirts.

1 garment [gɑːmənt] a piece of clothing

SPEAKING

6 Discussing complex topics → SB 18/5; ⟨G1⟩, G2; S30

MK

a) *You have agreed to record a short talk for the environmental awareness day at your partner school in England. Choose one of the topics below or create your own about sustainable fashion. Do some research and brainstorm ideas for your talk.*

- Fast fashion depends on bad pay and working conditions
- Not everybody can afford to pay more for good quality clothes
- Renting clothes has many benefits, but it"s too much trouble

b) *Write prompt cards for your talk. Practise and then record your talk. Present it in class.*

Tip

Record your talk, then (have a partner) listen to it and check: Do you use the correct words and pronunciation? Do you speak loudly and clearly? Is it easy to follow your talk? Take notes and record it again.

7 Sustainable consumption → SB 18/6; S29

LISTENING A2

a) *Listen to five speakers give their opinion on the sustainable consumption of fashion. Match the sentence parts to make statements about the speakers. There is* ***one*** *part you don't need.*

1. Evie …
2. Fynn …
3. Hazel …
4. Milo …
5. Audrey …

a) feels that other issues are more important than sustainable fashion.
b) likes to learn about and think carefully about sustainability issues.
c) now has far fewer things and buys very few new things.
d) has personal experience of the negative effects of the fashion industry.
e) supports the idea of sustainable fashion but cannot afford expensive clothes.
f) is an enthusiastic consumer of fashion.

b) *Listen again. Take notes to answer the questions.*

1. Evie mentions organic products, child labour and what three other issues?

____

____

2. In what three ways did Fynn dispose of things that he owned?

____

3. What point does Hazel make about countries where clothes are made?

____

4. What two benefits of the internet does Milo mention?

____

5. What two negative points does Audrey make about the fashion industry?

____

SPEAKING

c) *Discuss the sustainable consumption of fashion. Give your own opinion. Talk about ways to support it and what you will and won't do to consume fashion more sustainably.*

Word bank

to repair | to share | to sell | to regift | to upcycle | to swap | to think twice | to find out about | to research | second-hand | flea market | fashion label | trend | organic | fewer | less

MEDIATION

8 The right to repair → SB 18/7; S34

Your friend's phone isn't working. She is shocked to find out that it would be cheaper to buy a new phone than to repair her old one. You couldn't believe it either and did some research. Read the article, then write a message to your friend in German. Explain why many devices are not easy or possible to repair, what the Right to Repair *movement is and how the situation might change in the future.*

The right to repair

A A key way that people can reduce their ecological footprint is by making their electrical and electronic devices last longer. Replacing these things less frequently means fewer resources are needed, less CO_2 is generated and there is less electronic waste to dispose of (right now the world produces around 50 million tons of it per year). Most people agree that we cannot continue as if our planet had unlimited resources, but there"s just one problem: companies do not seem to be very interested in making their products easy to repair. All too often, repairing an item is impossible because of the way it has been designed. In other cases, manufacturers make it impossible for anybody but themselves to repair their products - often for a much higher price than it would cost to get the item repaired independently or to do it yourself.

B There are two main reasons for this. Firstly, companies understandably want to minimise their production costs in order to keep their selling prices low and their profits high. That might mean using production processes that make repair difficult or even impossible. Secondly, most companies have no real interest in your devices being repaired. Their profits come from you buying new items, and the more often the better!

C Increasingly, people are finding this unacceptable. It is not only bad for the environment, it is also bad for your bank account when, for example, you have to throw away an otherwise perfectly good tablet because the non-replaceable battery no longer holds a charge[1]. Or you have to dispose of a fridge just because it is impossible to buy a replacement for a broken shelf.

D It didn"t always use to be this way. Even in the quite recent past, many more devices were made in a way that anyone with a set of screwdrivers could fix them. The *Right to Repair* movement believes that companies ought to make sure that their products can easily be repaired when necessary, as they used to be. It also aims to require companies to make spare parts[2] easily available at fair prices.

E It can seem as though going against the interests of big businesses is an impossible task, but there have been some successes in getting governments to change regulations. In 2021 the UK introduced a law which requires companies to make spare parts available to consumers and independent repairers. However, this law does not cover smartphones and laptops, two of the items most frequently disposed of. The movement has also succeeded in getting some companies to change their ways, partly by getting more consumers to consider how long something is actually likely to last before they buy it. For example, 'consumer replaceable battery" has become a feature that some people now look for when choosing their next smartphone.

F Thanks to the *Right to Repair* movement, it could become common to buy devices expecting them to last a lot longer than they do today. Companies would start to think about how they can make products that last longer or can easily be repaired. Maybe more companies will offer their own repair services in the future or work together with workshops that do repairs.

1 to hold a charge [ˌhəʊld ə ˈtʃɑːdʒ] for a battery to last as long as it's supposed to **2** spare part [ˌspeə ˈpɑːt] an extra piece that can be used to replace a piece, especially in a machine

VOCABULARY

9 How and why I became a vegan

→ SB 21/1

a) *Harry is an influencer and explains in a post how and why he adopted a vegan diet. Put in the right words and change the form where necessary.*

aware | dairy product | diet | factor | fertiliser | to generate | pork | preferably | processing | resources | seasonal

My first step to becoming a vegan was becoming a vegetarian when I was 13. There were a number of ____________ behind that. One was having a holiday on a farm, seeing the cows and pigs and realising where our food comes from. That made me decide never to eat beef or ____________ again! Then I found out that animal farming uses a lot more ____________ than growing crops, and it ____________ a lot more CO_2, so I decided to stop eating all types of meat. Not too long after that, I became ____________ of the fact that ____________ are almost as bad for the environment as meat, and I decided to stop eating those too. My parents were fine about it and supported me when I switched to a 100 % plant-based ____________. There are still environmental issues with that too, of course, like growing crops with chemical ____________ and then transporting them long distances. I try to go for local, organic, ____________ vegan food, and ____________ stuff that hasn't been through a lot of ____________ before it gets to me.

b) *Share your thoughts about a vegan diet in a comment on Harry's post.*

GRAMMAR

10 ‹Organising a meal›

→ SB 21/3; ‹G3›

Jack and Amina want to organise a restaurant meal after an environmental activists' meeting. In your exercise book, rewrite their conversation with the ***substitute forms of to be able to, to have to*** *or* ***to be allowed to*** *instead of the modals.*

Amina: We **must** find a vegan restaurant.
Jack: I **couldn't** find one around here last time I tried.
Amina: We **needn't** go to an actual vegan restaurant.
It only **must** be a restaurant that can provide vegan options.
Jack: What time **may** we leave the meeting?
Amina: Last time we **could** leave when we wanted to. If we leave early,
we **can** reserve a table at the restaurant before everyone gets there.

GRAMMAR

11 A school announcement → SB 21/4; G4

a) *Complete this announcement on a school website with the modals **shall, might, ought to** and **would**. Use each modal once.*

Everyone agrees that we all ____________ do what we can to reduce the size of our ecological footprint, but what ____________ we do to make that happen as a school? We ____________ love to hear *your* ideas. If we work together as a team on this, we ____________ be able to make a real difference.

b) *Your school and your partner school in England both want to reduce their ecological footprint. Write an email to a group of students at your partner school in which you explain your ideas on how to reduce your ecological footprint and ask about their experiences. Include the modals **shall, might, ought to** and **would**.*

Word bank

to save resources | to consume less | energy-saving lights | renewable energy | greener forms of transport | e-bikes | recycling | to ban single-use water bottles | school garden | organic / locally-produced food | vegetarian / vegan options | to raise awareness

GRAMMAR

12 When I was your age … → SB 22/5; G4

a) *Complete part of a conversation between Ellen and her dad Mickey with a form of **used to**.*

Mickey: When I was younger, I ____________ care about the environment. I ____________ leave lots of lights on and I ____________ recycle anything.

Ellen: ____________ your family ____________ say anything about that?

Mickey: They ____________ criticise me for it sometimes, but I ____________ listen. And also, my parents' comments ____________ be more about saving money than about saving the environment.

Ellen: I see. I guess people just ____________ think about it like that.

b) *Imagine the world 50 years from now. People have finally understood that they need to take care of the Earth and live sustainably. You look back on your life today. Talk to a partner or record a voice message about how things **used to / didn't use to be** and what you **used to / didn't use to do**. What things do you do today that might be unacceptable in 50 years? Use the ideas below or come up with your own.*

to drive / own cars | to fly for holidays | to burn coal | food in plastic packaging | bottled water | food from places far away | to eat meat every day | rubbish in the sea | homes not energy efficient | air pollution | cheap clothes | solar panels

Useful phrases

used to think it was OK to … | didn"t use to care about … | used to be normal to …

VOCABULARY

13 Writing about greenwashing → SB 23/1

Ellen has written a text about consumerism and the environment for a school project. Suggest how she could improve some of her sentences so that they sound better. To do so, replace the parts in ***bold*** *by using words from ex. 1 on p. 23 in your book. You may need to change the form.*

1. 'Fairtrade' is **an official label** that promises acceptable working conditions and fair pay for farmers and workers in developing countries.

   ___

2. This product **has an extremely small ecological footprint**. After it has been thrown away, it **will slowly return to nature**.

   ___

3. A number of the company's **statements about this product's sustainability give a very false impression**.

   ___

4. The definition of this term has not been **recognised by the law**.

   ___

5. To do **shopping that isn't too harmful for the environment**, it can be helpful to read **the small text** on a product's packaging.

   ___

WRITING

14 Your turn: Online comment → SB 23/2

Choose one of the following quotations from the documentary "Beware of 'greenwashing'" *on p. 23 in your book. Write an online comment in which you say whether or not the statement matches your experience and your knowledge of this issue in Germany. Use your exercise book.*

1. "Polls[1] show that half of US consumers under thirty are willing to pay a premium[2] for products they consider eco-friendly."
2. "Today it suffices[3] to just slap some green paint on a product to call it 'green'."

WRITING

15 Cartoons → SB 23/3; S13

Choose one of the cartoons, then describe and analyse it. Explain the point that the cartoonist is trying to make.

"Yeah, it's all grown locally. Just not locally around here."

1 poll [pəʊl] survey ◯ 2 premium ['priːmiəm] an amount of money that is more than usual ◯ 3 to suffice [sə'faɪs] to be enough

Burning Sunlight

→ SB 26/5; S1, S2

A 3-7

Following the death of her activist mother, Zaynab Egal arrives in rural Devon. It's a world away from her home in Somaliland, a country that sees itself as independent, but isn't accepted as such, and may soon be no more than a desert. When she meets shy classmate Lucas Rowe, they discover they share a common cause: the climate crisis. They start a Friday for Future *group at their school and fight for their right to protest and be heard.*

A **LUCAS**

In the end there were only nine of us at the planning meeting for our Fridays for Future strike. I could tell Zaynab was disappointed, even though she tried hard to hide it. Aoife and Jack, a tall thin boy around fifteen, and a girl about the same age. No one from our class until, just as Zaynab was about to start, the doors flew open and the twins burst in.

"Ready, willing and able to save the planet!" said Poppy, breathlessly, pretending to salute Zaynab.

"God help us!" groaned Aoife. "The gruesome twosome."

"This is so cool, because we've been, like, freaking about climate change and we are really into activism," Daisy enthused.

"We made banners and placards and we were on Channel 4 News. The media loves twins," boasted Poppy.

"Who even cares?" Aoife interrupted, "and which one of you is which, anyway?"

"I'm Poppy! My hair's, like, blonder than Daisy's. See?"

Aoife snorted. "Name badges would be easier."

I could see Zaynab was beginning to get annoyed.

"Why are you here? Any of you? Why?" she asked.

"Like I said," started Poppy, "we really care about the planet and we want to stop climate change."

"Emergency," I said. "It's an emergency, now."

"We only eat organic. And we recycle. I mean like everything. We buy those huge bottles of shampoo and stuff because it's less plastic."

This was from a girl with big, round glasses, who said her name was Sophie-Ann. She was in Year Ten. While she was speaking, another girl from our class slunk into the room. Izzy Anderson. Even more shy than me.

"We use shampoo in a bar, like soap, so that's no plastic at all," Daisy said, smugly.

"Jeez!" Aoife stood up. "What even is this? Some kinda flipping competition? I only use planet friendly this and organic that, blah, blah, blah. It's all virtue signalling[1] rubbish. You're all consumers. You're consuming rubbish. They're marketing it to you to make you feel good. You don't even need to wash your hair. It's all just garbage like Jack says."

B Zaynab had that eagle look on her face.

Then she spoke. There was something in Zaynab's voice – a kind of energy – that made everyone else pay attention, even though we were the Juniors in the room.

"Why are you here?" she repeated. There was a short silence.

"Because I care," the tall, thin boy spoke. "I care and I don't want anybody to say that I didn't bother to do anything. That I let it all be destroyed. Because we are killing and poisoning[2] everything and we have got to make it all stop."

Zaynab nodded in approval.

"We need to do something to get people's attention. I mean," she looked round the room – "this is pathetic, right? Nine of us. Out of a total of six hundred and fifty."

1 virtue signalling ['vɜːtʃuː sɪɡnəlɪŋ] expressing your opinion in public to show that you are a good person **2** to poison ['pɔɪzn] to have a terrible effect on

"Less than two per cent." This was from the thin boy, whose name was Rudy Harris. "Dire."

"So what *are* we doing here?" asked Daisy.

"We are joining the Fridays for Future campaign. And we are going to stage a school strike. Next Friday." Zaynab's eyes flashed with excitement.

"Why don't you tell them why *you* are doing this, Zaynab?" I asked, shyly. "I'm here because of you and your story, really."

Zaynab took a deep breath and then she told us all about her mother's work. "It's really hard to explain what it is like to lose everything. I only know a bit about it because I've seen it. Families in a shack[3] made of corrugated iron[4] that gets scorching hot during the day. No water. No power. No loo[5]. No privacy. No safety."

Poppy and Daisy squeaked, "Euww."

"Imagine seeing your animals starving to death. Imagine leaving your house, your farm, and taking only the few things you can carry and then imagine walking further than going to the moors and back ten times to try to find food. And all because rich countries have been pumping out greenhouse gases without thinking what it does to us. You look outside and it's all green. You turn on your tap and you can drink the water that comes out of it. You can go to a proper loo and lock the door. Things you do here might not wreck your lives, but they destroy ours. That's the bit *you* don't get."

C When she had finished, she had a faraway look about her and I guessed she was back home in her head. We didn't know what to say. It was embarrassing. Then she seemed to snap back into our world and into a different kind of mood.

"I think we should occupy the space by the Town Hall. Nobody will see us if we do it outside school. It's too far from a main road. And, anyway, Greta[6] said it's best to be outside a government building."

Izzy was wide-eyed. "You mean, we don't go to school?"

"School strike! What do you think that means, brainbox?" Aoife's voice was full of contempt[7].

"Maybe we should get a permission?" said Daisy.

"No." Zaynab was very definite. "They might refuse. We just do it. This is a rebellion. Are you in or out?"

"I'm worried about getting in trouble," Izzy said, wringing her hands so that the knuckles showed white.

Aoife rolled her eyes. "Some rebel you'll be!"

"We need the media to take notice," said Rudy, "otherwise, it'll be a waste of time."

"You should film it," Sophie-Ann said and then, when she caught the look on Zaynab's face, "I mean, I will film it. Then we can post on Insta and TikTok."

"Great. Friday, then. Straight off the bus and into position outside the Town Hall. Tell everyone you can." Zaynab shut her notebook.

When they'd all gone, I asked Zaynab if she thought it was weird that everyone had let her be in charge, without any kind of challenge at all, when she was one of the youngest in the room.

She looked at me as if it had never occurred to her that it should be any other way.

I guess that was what made her a leader.

3 shack [ʃæk] very simple and small building ◯ **4** corrugated iron [kɒrəgeɪtɪd_ˈaɪən] a flat piece of metal that has a wave-like structure ◯ **5** loo [luː] toilet ◯ **6** Greta *here:* Greta Thunberg, a climate activist from Sweden ◯ **7** contempt [kənˈtemt] a strong feeling of having no respect for sb

Mrs Baldwin, the head teacher, has ended their protest outside the Town Hall and Zaynab has been called to her office.

D

ZAYNAB

"Did it not occur to you that the school as a whole might want to participate in your little event? Might it not have been a good idea to discuss this with your class teacher?"

Was she trying to suggest that the school would have backed us going on strike? In the street, in public? More likely she'd have allowed it in class or in the playground at breaktime. Out of sight. Pointless!

"It would have been a different thing," I replied. "Anyway, if you cared, you should have been doing it already. It should not be left to a person like me to organise."

She pursed her lips[8].

"It is not so simple, Zaynab. We have obligations[9] and duties[10], no matter what our private views might be."

"Well, there you go," I said.

"But we could possibly have found a way to support your initiative. You would have had many more people involved, made a bigger impact and a bigger story, and all without breaking rules."

"Making it a school thing would change it. I want people who care enough to just get up and do something. It's meaningless, otherwise," I said.

"But if only the most passionate get involved, you risk having a very small group with very little influence. You have to take people with you, Zaynab. You are very young to be learning this lesson, but it is an important one. There is a phrase – 'the lunatic fringe' – which is used to describe people who are extremists. I don't think you want to be part of that. Not if you really want to change the world."

I did not want to hear her weak vision of the world and of people who cared.

"No matter what may or may not be happening to our environment, you do still need an education, Zaynab, and that is what we are under an obligation to provide."

"An education for what? So that we can write about the death of the planet? So we can calculate how many days we have left? You aren't even telling the truth about what's actually happening."

E

Mrs Baldwin took a deep breath.

"There is a balance to be struck, Zaynab. Climate change plays a big part in the curriculum[11], especially if you choose to do geography for your GCSEs."

"But it should be in *everything*. Don't you get it? There are countries that won't exist and people who will die if you adults keep on pretending that nothing is happening or that it's not as bad as it is."

"We cannot frighten[12] people, Zaynab. There is nothing to be gained by frightening people when there is nothing you can give them to do with that fear. I cannot have a school filled with children too scared to sleep at night, too worried to eat or enjoy their childhood. The parents would not tolerate that, for a start."

I didn't see why she should wriggle out of this by blaming the parents.

"You have to do something. It is your job," I said, staring at her unflinchingly.

She sat back in her chair and closed her eyes. I could almost hear her counting to ten in her head.

"Very well. Here is my suggestion. Put a proposal to me about how we could be doing more than we already do and we will consider whether to take up these proposals. I am not promising anything, but can we agree that this is a way forward?"

I grunted. Was she wasting my time? Our time? We'd have to see.

I got up to go.

"You won't suspend the others, will you?"

She gave me a stony look.

"I await your proposals[13], Zaynab. You stand out, Zaynab, for all sorts of reasons, as I am sure you are only too aware. If I were you, I would make sure I stood out for the right reasons."

Her words echoed around my head for a long time. From her, they were a kind of threat but maybe I could turn them into a challenge.

From: Anthea Simmons, *Burning Sunlight*, 2021 (abridged)

8 to purse one's lips ['pɜːs wʌnz ˌlɪps] to bring your lips in a rounded shape because you don"t approve ○ **9** obligation [ˌɒblɪ'geɪʃn] responsibility ○ **10** duty ['djuːti] sth that you must do because it is part of your job, or because you feel it is the right thing to do ○ **11** curriuculum [kə'rɪkjələm] the subjects studied at a school and their contents ○ **12** to frighten ['fraɪtn] make sb afraid of sth ○ **13** proposal [prə'peʊzl] suggestion

READING

16 Understanding the story
→ SB 26/5; S1, S2

Read the novel extract. Somebody has written a news report about the events in the story for the school blog but most of the facts are wrong. Find the mistakes and write a corrected version in your exercise book.

> 9% of the school's students met for the Fridays for Future campaign. The group has no leader, but they agreed to protest outside the school after the end of the school day. Following the protest, all the people who were involved had to go to our head teacher's office. They have been asked to suggest how to reduce the school's ecological footprint. The head teacher has promised to do whatever the group suggests.

WRITING

17 Analysis: Characterisation
→ SB 26/5; S7

a) *Find and underline key sentences in the text which tell the reader about Zaynab's character, feelings and background.*

b) *Write a characterisation of Zaynab in your exercise book. What type of personality does she have? What does the extract tell the reader about her feelings, her background and her experiences? Use the information that you found in a).*

WRITING

18 Analysis: Narrative perspective
→ SB 26/5; S6

In the novel, Lucas and Zaynab take turns narrating the story. Comment on the author's decision to organise the novel in this way and have two first-person narrators. What possibilities does this offer compared to telling a story with just one first-person narrator or with a third-person narrator?

19 Options
→ SB 26/5; S17

*Choose **one** of the following tasks. Use your exercise book.*

WRITING

a) *Imagine that you are Zaynab. Write her proposal for Mrs Baldwin. Use this title:* How this school can do more to fight the climate emergency. *Include at least three practical suggestions, and explain how they would make a difference. Aim to persuade the reader to accept your proposals. Use a formal register and avoid emotional language.*

Useful phrases

With this proposal I want to … | Right now | In the future our school … | The school / teachers / students could … | Studies show that … | We can improve by … | I suggest / recommend we … | We should do more about … | Students should have a say in … | If we did … this would lead to …

b) *Write the missing scene which describes the protest and school strike. It must match the information in the extract, but you can invent all the other details. Decide on a narrator: Lucas or Zaynab.*

SPEAKING

c) *Imagine that you are Zaynab. Record a two-minute voice message to a cousin who still lives in Somaliland. Tell them about what has happened and how you feel about it.*

20 Reporting issues → SB 27/1; S8, S18

*Read a protest organiser's formal letter to a local TV channel. Look at the phrases in **bold** and use different colours to underline the ones that are suitable, too informal or rude. Then replace the phrases that are too informal or rude.*

Tip

Tips for writing in a formal register
- Use neutral adjectives and avoid informal words of all types.
- Use modals like *would*, *might* and *ought to*.
- Avoid exaggeration and emotional language.
- Use formal phrases.
- Use linking words.
- Use paragraphs and give the text a logical structure.

(1) **Hello people at Southwest TV News,**

(2) **I am writing concerning** a report on yesterday's local news programme at 5:45 p.m. about the climate protest that took place in Fenchester earlier in the day. (3) **I'm one of the bunch of people that organised it.** (4) **While I am grateful that** our protest was featured in your programme, I feel that the quality of the report (5) **was total rubbish**.

(6) **Firstly, the report said that** there were 'about a hundred' protesters. (7) **What a lie!** We counted the number carefully, and there were at least 180 persons at the peak of the protest.

(8) **Then the second thing** – although the reporter asked several members of the general public to give their opinions about the protest, there was no interview with anybody who was actually participating. (9) **Whose stupid idea was that?** (10) **We would have been very happy to** speak to your reporter, and we feel (11) **it was amazingly stupid that** we weren't given the opportunity to explain the issue and the reasons for our action.

(12) **Finally, the report missed mentioning** Fenchester Action on the Climate Crisis (FenACC), the organisers of the protest, (13) **even though this was clearly** written on a banner and in our leaflets. (14) **I reckon that this was *totally*** relevant information for your viewers, and it ought to have been mentioned instead of referring to us just as 'a local campaign group'.

For future reporting of our or any other organisation's protests, (15) **I hope that you will consider the points made above**.

(16) **Bye for now.**

Paige Edwards

21 Brainstorm ideas
→ SB 28 / Step 1

a) *Number these ideas for reducing waste from a school cafeteria from 1 to 7, in order of how useful you think they are. 1 is the most useful idea. Give reasons for your order.*

- ☐ Students bring boxes to take leftovers[1] home.
- ☐ Give leftover food to the local food bank.
- ☐ Set up a compost bin[2] on school grounds.
- ☐ Grow fruit and vegetables in a school garden.
- ☐ Students order lunches online the day before.
- ☐ Serve smaller portions (ask for more if you want it).
- ☐ Avoid buying food that has to be used very quickly.

b) *Who could be responsible for organising each of these actions? Make notes in your exercise book.*

22 Structure and write your letter
→ SB 28 / Step 3; S18

a) *Match the sentence halves to make complete sentences for a formal letter to the head of a school.*

1. We suggest the following …
2. We are writing to you concerning …
3. Firstly, …
4. Thank you in advance for …
5. We would especially like to draw your attention to the fact …
6. In conclusion, we would like to …
7. The current situation is …
8. We hope that you will consider …
9. As you may know …

a) reduce our school's ecological footprint by putting some of our ideas into practice.
b) unacceptable. No one cares or thinks about how much energy and resources we use.
c) we think that everyone should do their part to help the environment.
d) our school has quite a large ecological footprint.
e) that our school lunches are not sustainable.
f) changes: reduce waste, …
g) the ecological footprint of our school.
h) considering our suggestions.
i) our ideas to reduce the ecological footprint of our school.

b) *Decide for each phrase if it fits best with the introduction, main part or ending of a formal letter.*

c) *Complete the information about how to start and end a formal letter with the words below.*

Kind | Miss | sincerely | Mr | Sir or Madam | regards | Mrs

If you know the recipient's name, begin **Dear** ______________ … or **Ms** … Only use ______________ (= married woman) if you are sure the recipient prefers it. ______________ (= woman who isn't married) is not typically used any more. If you do not know the recipient's name, start **Dear** ______________. You can end with **Yours** ______________ but this may seem quite formal. Slightly less formal alternatives are **Best** ______________ and ______________ **regards**.

1 leftovers ['leftəʊvəz] food that hasn't been eaten after having a meal ○ 2 compost bin ['kɒmpɒst bɪn] a bin in which you put organic waste to turn into organic material over time

Can you …?

Stelle mithilfe des Bewertungsbogens im Beihefter auf Seite 25 fest, was du schon kannst oder noch üben musst.

Dealing with advertising

VOCABULARY

1 Working in advertising → 38/1

Nasreen works for an advertising agency[1] and writes about her job for a careers advice website. Complete her text with the words below. Change the form of the word where necessary.

bargain | brand | campaign | commercial | to launch | offer | print ad | customer | sale | sample | social media

Some people think this job is all about creating TV ______________ and ______________ for newspapers and magazines, but that's only part of it. ______________ is extremely important too, especially for ______________ new products and for developing the image of a ______________. It's also very good for finding out how ______________ react to marketing ______________. Part of my job is showing our clients[2] how to use free product ______________ to promote their products. Customers may not realise that 'buy one, get one free' ______________, 'everything must go' ______________ and that type of thing are often just another form of advertising. Just because somebody claims that something is a ______________ doesn't necessarily mean that it is!

VOCABULARY

2 Did you see the new ad? → SB 39/1

a) *For the careers advice website, Nasreen presents and analyses her latest ad to show what her job is about. Look at her ad and read the ad copy. What are the two claims of the slogan?*

b) *Complete her analysis of the ad.*

AIDA | attention | desire | eye-catching | interest | slogan | to take action | target group | visual

This ad is a good example of the ______________ formula. The most ______________ part of the ad is the ______________ – four bottles of fruit juice. Having attracted the ______________ of the ______________, the goal is now to increase their ______________ with a ______________ that has a double meaning. Overall, the ad aims to create a ______________ to drink this juice and to motivate people to ______________ by buying the product.

1 advertising agency ['ædvətaɪzɪŋ ˌeɪdʒnsi] a business that provides advertising services ○ **2** client [klaɪənt] sb who uses the services of a business

3 Planning an ad
→ SB 40/2; S14

VOCABULARY

a) *Look at the products and services that Nasreen is going to advertise next. Write down adjectives that can help to advertise each of them.*

1

2

3

4

5

6

WRITING

b) *Describe a possible target group for each of the products and services in a). Think about gender, age, interests, values and media use. Use your exercise book.*

c) *How can Nasreen reach these target groups? Match each of them with one or more suitable ways of advertising in the box below. Keep in mind the product or service you want to sell.*

ad on social media | flyers or brochures | TV commercials during prime time | free samples in a store | on an electronic billboard | influencer post on social media | print ads on public transportation

Across cultures

Unfortunately, advertising often relies on stereotypes, e.g. concerning gender roles, age, culture and body size. Have a closer look at the ads that you see in the next few days: Do they use stereotypes? If so, which ones?

SPEAKING

d) *Discuss your ideas in c) and explain why a specific way of advertising is a good choice for the particular target group and product or service you thought of.*

WRITING

4 Creating an ad
→ SB 40/3; S14

a) *Choose **one** of the products or services in ex. 3 and create an ad for it. Think of the AIDA formula.*

b) *Present your ad in class. Explain the choices you made in a). Give each other feedback.*

Tip

Before you start, answer these questions:
- What is special about your product or service?
- Who is your target group?
- How can you reach them?
- How can the advertisement attract them?

LISTENING

5 Advertising to teenagers → SB 42/2; S29

A8

a) *Listen to the start of a podcast about advertising to teenagers with Laurence Okafor, the director of an advertising agency[1] in London. Number the topics in the order that they are mentioned.*

- ☐ a rule about advertising food to children and teens
- ☐ different types of advertising
- ☐ how teenagers react to advertisements
- ☐ parents may influence their children's decisions
- ☐ reasons why teenagers are important to advertisers
- ☐ rules that advertisers have to follow
- ☐ teenagers may influence their parents' decisions
- ☐ the best ways to advertise to teenagers
- ☐ what teenagers spend their money on

b) *Are the statements true or false? Tick ✔ the correct answer. Correct the false ones in your exercise book.*

	true	false
1. Teenagers are attractive to advertisers because they can buy what they want.	☐	☐
2. It is difficult to predict what types of media a teenage target group uses.	☐	☐
3. Laurence says that teenagers are easier to persuade than adults.	☐	☐
4. Advertisers can't always predict how the Advertising Standards Authority will react.	☐	☐
5. Advertising agencies don't care what they sell or who they sell it to.	☐	☐
6. Laurence implies that teenagers' knowledge of products can be useful to parents.	☐	☐

6 Commercials: a cartoon →SB 42/3; S13

WRITING

a) *Describe and analyse the cartoon. Use your exercise book.*

Useful phrases

The setting is … | The caption says … | The cartoon's joke is that … | The cartoon shows / represents / suggests / refers to … | The cartoon conveys the message that …

SPEAKING

b) *In what ways could parents try to reduce the number of ads their children see? Discuss with a partner.*

Word bank

to limit | to control | to use a filter programme for children | to inform | to suggest | to warn | to turn off | to talk about … | to provide alternative …

"I even had commercials in my dream last night."

1 advertising agency ['ædvətaɪzɪŋ‿eɪdʒənsi] a business that provides advertising services

MEDIATION

7 Influencers and advertising → SB 44/5; S34

Your friend Eva loves to travel and to post about it on social media. A travel company based in the UK asked her to work for them as an influencer to advertise the UK to her German followers. Before she replies, she wants to find out more about influencer marketing in the tourist industry. You find this blog post. Record a voice message for Eva in German in which you answer these questions:

1. Why are influencers important in the travel and tourist industry?
2. What do travel influencers do?
3. What positive effects do companies expect?

Across cultures

The author mentions three different generations in the article, and uses the following terms:

- **(Baby) Boomers**: people born between 1946 and 1964
- **Millennials** (or **Gen Y**): born between 1981 and 1996
- **Gen Z**: born between 1997 and 2012

Find out more about these three generations. What terms are used to describe other generations? Say which generation you belong to and explain what makes yours stand out.

How influencer marketing is changing the travel industry

The scope of influencer marketing is growing. As more industries enter this marketing sphere, new trends are likely to emerge. One of the most recent trends has been the influx of destination bloggers and travellers.

How the conversation around travel has changed

For boomers and older generations, travel was not done frequently because their financial priorities were different. A majority of their spending was focused on large purchases such as houses and cars, instead of taking a trip. However, Millennials and Gen Z put more of an importance on experiences instead of traditional financial milestones, which reflects in their spending habits. As such, these are the demographics that are most likely to take trips and travel. Add in social media, and you have the perfect environment for travel influencers to thrive.

With so many younger, digitally savvy people eager to splurge on once-in-a-lifetime experiences, the travel industry has seen a period of massive growth. For people that are unable to take a vacation or long trip, seeing images and videos from other people's travels is a way for the user to escape – adding fuel to the fire for the travel influencer marketing industry.

What are travel influencers?

Travel influencers produce content focused primarily on going to new places and having experiences. While some started out as people who liked travel and showed it on social media, some travel influencers started going to new places because they saw it as an opportunity for their personal brand. Regardless of the intent, travel influencers have made their way into the mainstream of influencer marketing and brands are taking notice. For hospitality and tourism, this presents a giant opportunity to grow their industries with the help of influencers.

These types of influencers sell experiences as romantic or visionary and encourage their audiences to join in on their trip – or to take one of their own. Part of the power of travel influencers comes from their ability to make their followers feel connected to their experiences like they are encountering the same waterfall the same way the traveling influencers are. This connection shows a heightened level of engagement with travel influencer audiences, and reflects the trust that these audiences have in their influencers. By using travel influencers, travel agencies, country tourism departments and more can display their locations as desirable destinations for people with wanderlust and boost their popularity with travellers.

What's the right way to use travel influencers?

When used correctly, travel influencers have the potential to change the travel industry for good. As more people put an emphasis on authentic relationships with people that they trust, an influencer partnership can be used to create an engaging user experience that will inspire and encourage other users to do the same.

Maria Lewczyk, *Sideqik*, 2022 (abridged)

On these pages you are going to practise doing the types of tasks you will do in the ZP10 (*Zentrale Prüfung Klasse 10, Nordrhein-Westfalen*). You are also going to get some useful tips on how to deal with the tasks successfully.

1 Listening: Repair café

A 9 *Read the statements. Then listen to an interview for the* Birmingham Pulse *blog. A local blogger visits a community centre that hosts a repair café. She speaks to Josh, who is a volunteer there. While you are listening, tick ✔ the correct box. Then listen again and check your answers.*

1. Apart from the repair café, the community centre also offers …
   a) ☐ good coffee.
   b) ☐ many other activities.
   c) ☐ training courses.

2. When somebody brings something, the volunteers …
   a) ☐ can almost always repair it.
   b) ☐ sometimes repair it.
   c) ☐ only show people how to repair it themselves.

3. Smartphones are …
   a) ☐ impossible to repair today.
   b) ☐ easier to repair than laptops.
   c) ☐ the most common item brought to the café.

4. If part of your item needs to be replaced, the volunteers …
   a) ☐ can't help you.
   b) ☐ have everything you need there.
   c) ☐ offer support in finding it.

5. Josh says the repair café …
   a) ☐ helps local businesses.
   b) ☐ may be bad for local businesses.
   c) ☐ has no effect on local businesses.

6. Josh says the main benefits are helping the environment and …
   a) ☐ having fun.
   b) ☐ saving money.
   c) ☐ learning new skills.

7. Josh founded the repair café because …
   a) ☐ he saw one in another place.
   b) ☐ he thought it would be fun.
   c) ☐ his town really needed one.

8. The repair café happens …
   a) ☐ every weekend.
   b) ☐ when the volunteers want to do it.
   c) ☐ 12 times a year.

Tip

Before you start listening, read through the task first to get an overview:
- What might be the topic of the audio?
- What will you need to focus on while listening? If you're not sure about one of your answers the first time, just leave it out and continue listening. You can always come back to it in the second round.

In the final exam you can only listen twice. However, to practise you can listen more often if you need to.

2 Reading: Sustainable fashion

What is Sustainable Fashion? Your Go-To Guide

What does 'sustainable fashion' mean?

Sustainable fashion refers to pieces of clothing and accessories that are produced and / or accessed[1] in an ecologically and socially responsible way. The reason that the word "accessed" is in this sustainable fashion definition is that the term should not be limited to making or buying new things. While sustainability marketing campaigns have led us to believe that we can buy our way to sustainability, it's not that simple. We can certainly choose to shop in a more sustainable way, but getting involved with sustainable fashion does not require buying anything new. Wearing what you have, shopping second-hand, and swapping with or borrowing from friends are other ways to participate in the sustainable fashion movement that doesn't require the production or purchasing of anything new.

Why is sustainable fashion so important?

Fashion has been causing harmful environmental and social impacts for a long time. What we know as sweatshops today first appeared in England during the Industrial Revolution, and these early factories depended on coal. Plus, the industrialization of textiles created a larger demand for cotton, which was a major driver for slavery. The relatively recent rise of fast fashion, though, has been a huge part of problems in fashion today like modern-day slavery, toxic[2] pollution, and excessive carbon emissions. *What is fast fashion?* Fast fashion is trendy, cheap fashion that is produced very quickly in large quantities[3].

Why, exactly, is fast fashion so bad?

The fast fashion model is built on an endless cycle of overproduction and overconsumption. Cheap prices from fast fashion brands are *only* made possible because these brands produce in huge quantities. While the companies don't make much profit from each piece of clothing, they are able to profit hundreds of millions or even billions because they produce so much. And, because fast fashion brands produce in such large quantities, they are able to negotiate[4] prices down with factories. These negotiations[5] keep wages and safety standards low.

The rise of fast fashion has also started a "race to the bottom" for the industry as a whole, as brands try to produce clothes as cheaply and quickly as possible in order to offer trendy pieces at low prices. Here are some statistics to paint the picture of the fashion industry today:

- Textile production was responsible for 1.2 billion tons of greenhouse gas emissions in 2015 alone. This is more than the emissions from all international flights and maritime[6] shipping combined.
- The fashion industry depends on non-renewable energy. The vast majority of clothing – nearly 70 % – is made from polyester or other synthetic fabrics from non-renewable resources.
- Clothes made from synthetic materials are responsible for as much as 35 % of global microplastic pollution.
- One garbage truck's worth of textiles is landfilled or burned every single second.

What are the benefits of sustainable fashion?

Cleaning up the fashion supply chain can also mean reducing pollution a lot in many communities around the world. Sourcing textiles for fashion from regenerative materials can put us on a path to restoring the planet and our relationship to the land. And with about 430 million people to work directly or indirectly for the fashion and textile industries, improving the supply chains of the fashion industry can mean significant improvements in the lives of many.

Elizabeth Joy, *Conscious Life & Style* website, 2021 (abridged and adapted)

1 to access ['ækses] to be able to use sth ○ **2** toxic ['tɒksɪk] causing death or illness if it gets into one's body ○ **3** quantity ['kwɒntɪti] an amount of sth ○ **4** to negotiate [nɪ'gəʊʃieɪt] to try to agree on sth by having a formal discussion ○ **5** negotiation [nɪˌgəʊʃi'eɪʃn] formal discussion in order to agree on sth ○ **6** maritime ['mærɪtaɪm] relating to the sea and ships

You are doing research for a school project on the environmental impact of different industries. You have found a relevant article on a sustainable lifestyle website. Read the article. Tick ✓ the correct box and give one piece of evidence by quoting short passages from the text.

1. In the text, 'sustainable fashion' means
   a) ☐ buying sustainably-made clothes.
   b) ☐ buying fewer, better-quality clothes.
   c) ☐ reducing the environmental impact of clothing in a number of ways.

   ____

   ____

2. Advertisers have created an idea of sustainability that is …
   a) ☐ totally false.
   b) ☐ misleading.
   c) ☐ very helpful.

   ____

   ____

3. Industrial fashion production has had very damaging effects since …
   a) ☐ it began.
   b) ☐ demand increased.
   c) ☐ the arrival of fast fashion.

   ____

   ____

4. The textile industry was …
   a) ☐ what started slavery.
   b) ☐ a significant cause of slavery.
   c) ☐ an indirect result of slavery.

   ____

   ____

5. Fast fashion makes a lot of money because …
   a) ☐ a lot of it is sold.
   b) ☐ the profit on each item is quite high.
   c) ☐ marketing and selling costs are low.

   ____

   ____

6. Factory workers' pay is bad because …
   a) ☐ it is impossible to work fast enough to earn much.
   b) ☐ the brands and factories agree on low production costs.
   c) ☐ the brands also own the factories.

   ____

   ____

7. Most clothing is …
   a) ☐ made with non-natural materials.
   b) ☐ transported by air or by sea.
   c) ☐ burned after it is thrown away.

   ____

   ____

8. Sustainability in this industry will also …
   a) ☐ create better jobs.
   b) ☐ produce nicer clothes for everyone.
   c) ☐ improve local environments.

   ____

   ____

Tip

Skim the text: What is it about? Then read the questions and highlight relevant key words. Next, scan the text for passages that are relevant to answer the questions. Can you find some of the key words you highlighted in the questions? These words may indicate a relevant text passage. But be careful: the questions very often use alternatives to key words in the text. To shorten your quotations, leave out a few words or sentences: "Cleaning up the fashion supply chain […] to the land." (ll. 40–42)

VOCABULARY

1 Digital world → SB 46/2

Cross out the word that doesn't fit. Say why the other words go together.

Reason:

1. laptop | controller | tablet | smartphone ____________
2. application | AR goggles | VR headset | console ____________
3. to enhance | to immerse oneself in sth | to scan | to replace ____________
4. virtual reality | augmented reality | virtual tour | three-dimensional ____________

2 Review: virtual tours of Edinburgh → SB 47/4

VOCABULARY

a) *Finley is a performing arts blogger. Complete his review of a few virtual tours of Edinburgh during the Fringe Festival. Change the form of the word where necessary.*

dimension | disclaimer | from the comfort of | hike | image | in person | to interact | peek | real-life | virtual | written

I've always wanted to visit Edinburgh, especially during the Fringe Festival (the world's biggest arts festival, in case you didn't already know). Of course, my first choice would be to go there ____________ but it's a 10-hour train journey from my home in Cornwall! So then I thought, what about a ____________ tour? I've been on some amazing virtual ____________ in wild places ____________ my sofa. Maybe it would work for Edinburgh during the festival. The first 'tour' I tried was just a moving ____________ from somebody's phone with no sound. That kind of thing should come with a ____________: 'Warning: This tour is rubbish'! But then I found some much better ones with guides. Some seem to have a semi- ____________ script with lots of interesting information, and that really adds an extra ____________ to the tour. You get a few quick ____________ at street performers too, but there's much more to the festival than that. I also found that during the festival you can watch some of the stage performances online, but of course you won't be able to ____________ with anyone. For me, the main effect of these virtual tours was to make me want to have the ____________ experience even more!

SPEAKING MK

b) *Discuss your answers to these questions.*

1. What are the advantages and disadvantages of virtual tours?
2. Can you really experience a place, a culture or an event virtually? Explain why / why not.
3. What are the characteristics of good and bad virtual tours?

Unit 2 The digital age

1 My digital life → SB 51/2

VOCABULARY

a) *Aly read an article about teens and social media. There were some parts she didn't like. Complete her letter to the editor. Change the form of the verbs where necessary.*

brand | to embrace | footprint | to foster a mindset | to miss out | to perceive | to relate to | temptation | to get (= to understand) | to be willing to

Dear Editor,

I would like to comment on your article "Help! Our teens are addicted[1]" published on 2nd February. The article only described the negative sides of social media. I think the way I ________________ digital technology and my digital ________________ are quite typical for someone of my age (16). For example, I love that I can keep in touch with my friends so easily. Also, digital technology gives me more choices in what I do. Last night my parents were watching a show on TV. I ________________ watch it with them, but I got bored and took out my phone. My parents said I should focus on one thing at a time, but why should I keep doing something I don't like? That doesn't mean I'm "addicted". 'I think my generation just needs a little more excitement and options sometimes, and I don't think older generations can always ________________ how we live our lives. But I understand your argument that ________________ too much technology can become an issue. I agree that it ____________________________ of being available at all times. Even when I'm doing other things, I often feel the ________________ to check social media so that I don't ________________ on the latest gossip. For my brother, it's all about the gadgets. He is more interested in what ________________ of phone people have than in social media. I don't ________________ it, but it's his life ... As you see, it's not that simple. We all use our phones and social media in different ways and I wish your article would have taken this into account.

Aly Doukas

MK

b) *Track your own digital media use for a day. Make a grid in which you make notes on:*

device | app or game used | activity | purpose | time

SPEAKING

c) *How do you feel about your result? If you're okay with it, what advice would you give to a friend who isn't? If you're not okay with the result, what can you do to make a change?*

Tip

A few ideas to make changes: charge your phone away from your bed; don't reply to a new message right away; avoid using your phone right after waking up; do something without the help of an app (e.g. find your way to a new place) or set a time limit for an app you want to use less. Change is hard, so go easy on yourself!

1 addicted [ə'dɪktɪd] having an addiction

GRAMMAR

2 ⟨An online course⟩ → SB 53/3; ⟨G6⟩

*Complete the conversation between Aly and her mother, who works as an energy consultant[1]. Choose the best **verb form** to fit the context. Where both fit well, choose the **one** that you prefer for the situation.*

Ms Doukas: I've got some news. **I'm going / I'll go** back to school! Well, in a way.

Aly: Wow! What **do you / are you going to** study?

Ms Doukas: It's a bit difficult to explain. **I'll try / I'm trying** to keep it simple. Soon all rented[2] homes in the UK **are having to / will have to** meet new environmental standards, and thousands of people **are going to be / are being** needed to carry out environmental tests. **I'm starting / I start** a training course that **will lead / is leading** to a qualification in carrying out these tests. I think it **will be / is going to be** a useful extra skill to have in my job.

Aly: So how **is that affecting / will that affect** work? **Are you going to take / Do you take** time off?

Ms Doukas: **I won't need / I'm not needing** to. **I'm going to do / I'm doing** the whole thing online in the evenings.

Aly: **Will that be / Is that going to be** very different to doing it in person?

Ms Doukas: The tutor says she **expects / is expecting** us to interact during the class, so in many ways it **will be / is going to be** very similar. The first lesson **will start / starts** at 6 o'clock on Monday evening, but **it'll be recorded / it's going to be recorded**, so **I'll be able to / I'm going to be able to** watch it later if I need to.

Aly: When **does the course end / is the course going to end**?

Ms Doukas: The lessons **are finishing / finish** after three weeks, but then **I'm doing / I do** some tests for the practical part.

GRAMMAR

3 Looking into my future → SB 53/4; G7, G8

a) *Use the **future progressive** and the **future perfect** to finish six sentences about your future.*

1. In 50 years' time … ______
2. By the time I'm 25 … ______
3. By the time I finish school … ______
4. When I'm 20 years old … ______
5. This time next year … ______
6. By next September … ______

b) *Ask each other questions about your future.*

Start: Will you have moved out in five years' time?
– No, I won't. But I'll have been to many other countries …

1 energy consultant ['enədʒi kənˌsʌltnt] sb who suggests cost-effective ways to improve the use of energy ○ 2 rented [rentɪd] sth for which you pay rent

VOCABULARY

4 The world as seen in stock[1] photos → SB 56/3

Complete the missing words in the online article.

Stock photo websites are extremely useful for the media industry. They e _ a _ l _ writers and editors to choose from hundreds of thousands of _ m _ g _ _ and find just the right one. Whether you want a p _ r _ _ _ _ t of a famous person for a news article, a striking image to illustrate a website or any other type of photo for any other reason, you will find a huge _ a r _ _ _ y to choose from for minimal cost. However, the criticism that stock photos cause _ o t _ n _ _ _ l harm is becoming louder. This is _ a r _ i c _ _ _ _ l y true for the many stock photos which show smiling, happy people doing everyday activities in homes, offices etc. These images present themselves as a r _ f _ _ c t _ _ _ of real life, but of course they are anything but that. They use professional models, make-up and carefully posed scenes to perpetuate stereotypes and a h o _ _ g _ n _ z _ _ world. The images have often been extremely r _ t o _ _ h _ _ or _ l t _ r _ d in some other way, and it is sometimes hard to find a suitable photo with s _ b j _ _ _ _ who are not white. This may make people who don't fit the stereotypes feel i _ _ d _ q u _ _ _. It would be nice to see more stock photos that celebrate people's individuality as o p _ _ _ _ d to the unreal world of the stock photographer's imagination.

Media skills

Stock photo websites sell the right to use "pre-made" photos, illustrations and videos to companies and private persons. It's often much faster, cheaper and easier than to hire a photographer or illustrator yourself. Most of the photos you can find online are stock photos. Only a few are Creative Commons licence photos, which means you can use them for free for certain purposes (e.g. in a presentation for school if you name the source).

GRAMMAR

5 ‹My favourite stock photo website› → SB 56/4; ‹G9›

*Put the sentences together using **defining** (= necessary information) or **non-defining** (= unnecessary information) **relative clauses**. Remember to put a comma before a non-defining relative clause.*

1. I use a stock photo site called MonsterStock. It says it has more than 400 million images.

____

2. I was looking for a stock photo. It shows some teenagers having fun.

____

3. My first search was for 'teenagers having fun'. It had nearly 200,000 results.

____

4. All together, they probably show more than the number of teenagers. They are having fun right now in real life!

____

1 stock [stɒk] a supply of sth that is available for sale or use

GRAMMAR

6 Everything seems perfect → SB 56/5; G10

*In your exercise book, copy and complete the sentences with a **non-defining relative clause which comments on the whole sentence**. Use the clue in brackets or your own idea. You can use the following phrases, more than once if you need.*

which is … | which means … | which makes … | which can … | which is why …

1. Images of 'perfect' people are everywhere online … (How does that make other people feel?)
2. Many of the people in stock photos are models … (How does that affect the photos?)
3. Software to edit photos is easy to use … (How does that affect retouching photos?)
4. Celebrities often post retouched photos of themselves … (When is this fine / not fine?)
5. Social media is a big part of many people's lives … (What does this mean we see a lot of?)
6. Many people compare themselves with social media photos … (How does that make them feel?)

GRAMMAR

7 Is it OK to post it? → SB 57/7; G11

a) *Match the photos with the posts and choose **where**, **when** or **which** to complete them.*

A class photo

B selfie

C holiday photo

D photo from a search engine

☐ 1. Here's me with my besties[1] Fran and Carmela **where / when / which** we were out and about yesterday. I can't remember **where / when / which** I bought that awful hat, but I won't shop there again! It's not something **where / when / which** I'd usually wear, but it was really cold **where / when / which** we were. Brrrr!

☐ 2. Here's what I was doing last Saturday night **where / when / which** most of you were asleep. It's the place in this town **where / when / which** all the really cool people go to have fun. Paaaaaarty!

☐ 3. I was at my little sister's school **where / when / which** her class photo was taken! I think it's a really cute picture so had to share it here **where / when / which** all of you can see it!

☐ 4. This is a pic I took **where / when / which** I was in New York last year. Can you work out **where / when / which** I was at the time? I think New York is a city **where / when / which** is great for a visit, but it's not a place **where / when / which** I'd like to live. Too hectic for me!

MK

b) *For each photo in a), discuss whether posting it online is OK or not and on what this depends.*

Useful phrases

to ask for permission | to show sb in an unattractive way | to use Creative Commons license photos | to own the rights | to be old enough | to have created sth yourself | to show illegal activity | to ruin sb

1 bestie ['besti] short for 'best friend'

MEDIATION

8 Insurance for gamers → SB 58/10; S34

Your friend from England just started getting into esports. She found a German article about the topic but has problems understanding everything. She is confused about why a fitness trainer works with gamers and wants to know if he gives any advice on how to become a successful esports gamer. Read the interview and answer her questions in an English email.

Fabian Broich, 30, war Fußballprofi – jetzt arbeitet er als Fitness- und Mentaltrainer im E-Sport. Der Head of Performance sagt, er sei eine Art Lebensversicherung für die Gamerinnen und Gamer.

Mit welchen Vorurteilen haben Sie es zu tun?

Fabian Broich: Es gibt das Klischee, dass man die Gamer aus dem Keller holen muss, wo sie sich nur von Tiefkühlpizza und Energydrinks ernähren. Und dass alle richtig ungenießbare Charaktere sind. Und diese Typen gibt es auch.

Die Klischees stimmen?

Broich: Manchmal habe ich den Eindruck, dass die Gamer wenig von der „Schule des Lebens" mitbekommen haben. Meine Aufgabe ist es – um im Bild zu bleiben –, sie aus dem Keller zu holen. Manche haben wirklich kaum oder gar kein Bewusstsein für ihren Körper und wie das mit der Leistung zusammenhängt. Viele glauben zum Beispiel, sie müssten immer mehr zocken, um mit den Besten mitzuhalten. Das führt aber langfristig zum Burn-out.

Was macht man als Head of Performance?

Broich: Wenn ich als Head of Performance dazukomme, ist die Frage: Bin ich krank, wenn ich einen Mentalcoach habe? Nein. Es geht um Optimierung. Ich bin eine Art Lebensversicherung für die Spieler. Wenn die Leistung nicht stimmt, kann das schnell zum Karriereende führen. Ich möchte ihnen dabei helfen, ihre Leistung konstant abzurufen.

Können Sie das konkretisieren?

Broich: Nehmen wir zum Beispiel Manuel Neuer. Der hat 99 Prozent seiner maximalen Leistung erreicht. Er ist psychisch so fit, dass er selbst an einem schlechten Tag 70 bis 80 Prozent dieser Leistung abrufen kann. Bei E-Sportlern ist das oft nicht so. Sie sind weder an ihrer Leistungsgrenze noch sind sie mental so gefestigt, um auch unter Druck ihre Leistung abzurufen.

Wie können Sie helfen?

Broich: Es gibt vier Säulen, die ich meinen Spielern beibringen möchte: Schlafen, Ernährung, Bewegung und mentale Gesundheit. Meistens fange ich beim Thema Schlafen an. Aus meiner Erfahrung haben 70 Prozent der E-Sportler Schlafprobleme.

Auch so ein Klischee.

Broich: Viele gehen zu spät ins Bett und schlafen zu wenig. Ich zeige ihnen, wie positiv sich gesunder Schlaf auf die Leistung auswirkt. Vor Mitternacht ins Bett gehen und mindestens acht Stunden schlafen – das ist wichtig für die Leistungsfähigkeit. Die professionellen Gamer merken einen schnellen Effekt, was sehr wichtig ist, denn das kennen sie schon vom Spielen: direkte und schnelle Belohnungen für gute Leistungen. Bei den anderen drei Säulen muss ich länger dranbleiben, bis sich ein positiver Effekt einstellt.

Wie gehen Sie da vor?

Broich: Ich will wissen, was die Spielenden für Ziele haben und was sie bereits wissen. Danach erstelle ich Ernährungs-, Tages- und Wochenpläne. Vorher haben die Spieler oft sechs Stunden am Stück trainiert. Ich sage dann: Vielleicht ist es sinnvoller dreimal zwei Stunden zu spielen. Ich kenne die Situation der Spieler, bin selbst mit 21 Jahren von zu Hause ausgezogen, um professioneller Fußballer zu werden. Von daher versuche ich, für die Spieler wie ein großer Bruder zu sein.

Fabian Held, *Die Zeit*, 2021 (adaptiert)

SPEAKING **9**

A presentation on a video game

→ SB 58/11; S30

Give a three-minute presentation on a famous video game or a video game you enjoy playing. In your presentation, explain how the game works, why it is so popular and / or why you like it.

VOCABULARY **10**

Negative emotions

→ SB 59/2

Complete Jason's comment on a social media post about cyberbullying. Change the form of the verb where necessary.

to give up | embarrassed | to feel sick | to get away with | to feel sorry for | helpless | to cry | to panic | rude | shocked | to stand up for | bad

It got so bad that I ____________ to my stomach every time I looked at my phone. And I started to ____________ about seeing those guys at school every day. I wished it would stop, but I was too ____________ to tell anyone. I was ____________ to change it and I just ____________. Then one day my sister found me ____________ about the latest nasty post. She was ____________ that the bullies ____________ it for so long, and made me agree to tell my teachers. Now I realise it's the bullies who should feel ____________, not the person who is being bullied. Looking back, I ____________ myself. I'm annoyed with myself. Why did I accept the bullies being ____________ and horrible to me? Why didn't I ____________ myself more? Why didn't I tell somebody earlier? I'll never let it happen again.

VOCABULARY **11** MK

Film vocabulary

→ SB 59/3; S15

Complete the mind map with useful vocabulary for a film analysis.

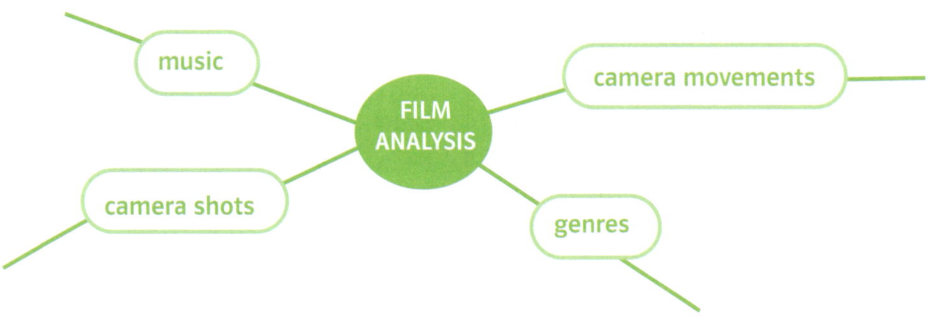

A 10–13

One of us is lying

→ SB 62/7; S1, S2

Bronwyn meets Simon, another student at her high school, on the way to detention. Simon has an app, About That, on which he posts gossip about other students.

A

Bronwyn
Monday, September 24, 2:55 p.m.

A sex tape. A pregnancy scare. Two cheating scandals. And that's just this week's update. If all you knew of Bayview High was Simon Kelleher's gossip app, you'd wonder how anyone found time to go to class.

"Old news, Bronwyn," says a voice over my shoulder. "Wait till you see tomorrow's post."

Damn. I hate getting caught reading About That, especially by its creator. I lower my phone and slam my locker shut. "Whose lives are you ruining next, Simon?"

Simon falls into step beside me as I move against the flow of students heading for the exit. "It's a public service," he says with a dismissive wave. "You tutor Reggie Crawley, don't you? Wouldn't you rather know he has a camera in his bedroom?"

I don't bother answering. Me getting anywhere near the bedroom of perpetual stoner[1] Reggie Crawley is about as likely as Simon growing a conscience[2].

"Anyway, they bring it on themselves. If people didn't lie and cheat, I'd be out of business." Simon's cold blue eyes take in my lengthening steps. "Where are you rushing off to? Covering yourself in extracurricular glory?"

I wish. As if to provoke me, an alert crosses my phone: *Mathlete[3] practice, 3 p.m., Epoch Coffee.* Followed by a text from one of my teammates: *Evan's here.*

Of course he is. The cute Mathlete – less of an oxymoron than you might think – seems to only ever show up when I can't.

"Not exactly," I say. As a general rule, and especially lately, I try to give Simon as little information as possible. We push through green metal doors to the back stairwell, a dividing line between the original Bayview High and its bright, airy new wing. Every year more wealthy families get priced out of San Diego and come fifteen miles east to Bayview, expecting that their tax dollars will buy them a nicer school experience than popcorn ceilings and scarred linoleum.

Simon's still following me when I reach Mr. Avery's lab on the third floor, and I half turn with my arms crossed. "Don't you have someplace to be?"

"Yeah. Detention," Simon says, and waits for me to keep walking. When I reach towards the knob instead, he starts laughing. "You're kidding me. You too? What's your crime?"

"I'm wrongfully accused," I mumble, and pull the door open quickly. Three other students are already seated, and I pause to take them in. Not the group I would have predicted. Except one.

Nate Macauley leans back in his chair and smirks at me. "You make a wrong turn? This is detention, not student council."

He should know. Nate's been in trouble since fifth grade, which is right around the time we last spoke. The gossip mill tells me he's on probation[4] with Bayview's finest for ... something. It might be a DUI[5]; it might be drug dealing. He's a notorious supplier, but my knowledge is purely theoretical.

"Save the commentary." Mr. Avery checks something off on a clipboard and closes the door behind Simon. High arched windows lining the back wall send triangles of afternoon sun splashing across the floor, and faint sounds of football practice float from the field behind the parking lot below.

B

I take a seat as Cooper Clay, who's holding a crumpled piece of paper like a baseball, whispers "Heads up, Addy" and throws it toward the girl across from him. Addy Prentiss blinks, smiles uncertainly, and lets the ball drop to the floor.

The classroom clock was slowly moving toward three, and I followed its progress with a helpless feeling of injustice. I shouldn't even *be* here. I should be at Epoch Coffee, flirting awkwardly with Evan Neiman over Math questions.

Mr. Avery is a give-detention-first, ask-questions-never kind of guy, but maybe there's still time to change his mind. I clear my throat and start to raise my hand until I notice Nate's

1 stoner ['stəʊnə] sb who smokes cannabis a lot **2** to grow a conscience [ˌɡrəʊ‿ə 'kɒnʃns] to develop a sense for what's right and wrong **3** Mathlete ['mæθliːt] student who takes part in Math competitions **4** probation [prə'beɪʃən] period of time in which a criminal must behave well so that they are not sent to prison **5** DUI stands for 'Driving Under the Influence' (of alcohol or other drugs)

smirk broadening. "Mr. Avery, that wasn't my phone you found. I don't know how it got into my bag. *This* is mine," I say, waving my iPhone in its melon-striped case.

Honestly, you'd have to be clueless to bring a phone to Mr. Avery's lab. He has a strict no-phone policy and spends the first ten minutes of every class searching through backpacks like he's head of airline security and we're all on the watch list. My phone was in my locker, like always.

"You too?" Addy turns to me so quickly, her blond shampoo-ad hair swirls around her shoulders. She must have been surgically removed from her boyfriend, Jake Riordan, in order to show up alone. "That wasn't my phone either."

"Me three," Cooper declares. He and Addy exchange surprised looks, and I wonder how this is news to them when they're part of the same clique. Maybe überpopular people have better things to talk about than unfair detentions.

"Somebody has played a trick on us!" Simon leans forward with his elbows on the desk, looking spring-loaded and ready for fresh gossip. His gaze wanders over all four of us, clustered in the otherwise empty classroom, before settling on Nate. "Why would anybody want to trap a bunch of students with mostly spotless records in detention? Seems like the sort of thing that, oh, I don't know, a guy who's here all the time might do for fun."

I look at Nate, but can't picture it. Getting us detention sounds like work, and everything about Nate – from his messy dark hair to his ratty leather jacket – screams *Can't be bothered*[6]. Or yawns it, maybe. He meets my eyes but doesn't say a word, just tips his chair back even farther. Another millimeter and he'll fall right over.

Cooper sits up straighter, a frown crossing his Captain America face. "Hang on. I thought this was just a mix-up, but if the same thing happened to all of us, it's somebody's stupid idea of a prank. And I'm missing *baseball practice* because of it." He says it like he's a heart surgeon being kept from a lifesaving operation.

Mr. Avery rolls his eyes. "Save it for another teacher. I'm not buying it. You all know the rules against bringing phones to class, and you broke them." He gives Simon an especially sour glance.

C Teachers know About That exists, but there's not much they can do to stop it. Simon only uses initials to identify people and never talks openly about school. "Now listen up. You're here until four. I want each of you to write a five-hundred-word essay on how technology is ruining American high schools. Anyone who can't follow the rules gets another detention tomorrow."

"What do we write with?" Addy asks. "There aren't any computers here." Most classrooms have Chromebooks, but Mr. Avery, who looks like he should have retired[7] a decade ago, is a holdout.

Mr. Avery crosses to Addy's desk and taps the corner of a lined yellow notepad. We all have one. "Explore the magic of longhand writing. It's a lost art."

Addy's pretty, heart-shaped face is a mask of confusion. "But how do we know when we've reached five hundred words?"

"Count," Mr. Avery replies. His eyes drop to the phone I'm still holding. "And hand that over, Miss Rojas."

"Doesn't the fact that you're confiscating my phone *twice* give you pause? Who has two phones?" I ask. Nate grins, so quick I almost miss it. "Seriously, Mr. Avery, somebody was playing a joke on us."

Mr. Avery's snowy mustache twitches in annoyance and he extends his hand with a beckoning motion. "*Phone*, Miss Rojas. Unless you want a return visit." I give it over with a sigh

6 can't be bothered [ˌkɑːnt bi ˈbɒðəd] too lazy or tired to do sth you should or are expected to do ◯ **7** to retire [rɪˈtaɪə] to stop working because of age as he looks disapprovingly at the others. "The phones I took from the rest of you earlier are in my desk. You'll get them back after detention." Addy and Cooper exchange amused glances, probably because their actual phones are safe in their backpacks.

Mr. Avery throws my phone into a drawer and sits behind the teacher's desk, opening a book as he prepares to ignore us for the next hour. I pull out a pen, tap it against my yellow notepad, and contemplate the assignment. Does Mr. Avery really believe technology is ruining schools? That's a pretty exaggerated statement to make over a few smuggled phones. Maybe it's a trap and he's looking for us to challenge him instead of agree.

I glance at Nate, who's bent over his notepad writing *computers suck* over and over in block letters.

It's possible I'm overthinking this.

A few minutes later, Mr. Avery has to go outside for a few minutes because of a car accident that happens right in front of the building. During this time, Simon has an allergic reaction because someone put peanut[8] *oil in his drinking water. Due to unfortunate events (that may or may not have been a coincidence), Simon can't be saved. He dies at the hospital. Now the police are trying to find out who put the peanut oil in Simon's cup during detention.*

D **Addy**
Sunday, September 30, 2:05 p.m.

Detective Wheeler turns the laptop so it's facing me. I'm not sure what I'm looking at, but it seems like some kind of a blog, with the About That logo front and center. I give her a questioning look, and she says, "This is the admin panel Simon used to manage content for About That. The text below last Monday's date stamp are his latest posts."

I lean forward and start to read.

First time this app has ever featured good-girl BR, who has the school's most perfect academic record. Except she didn't get that A in chemistry through hard work, except if that's how you define stealing tests from Mr. C's Google Drive. Someone call Yale …

On the opposite end of the spectrum, our favorite criminal NM's back to doing what he does best: making sure the entire school is as high as it wants to be. Pretty sure that's a probation violation there, N.

MLB plus CC equals a whole lot of green next June, right? Seems like Bayview's southpaw[9] will make a splash[10] in the major leagues … but don't they have some pretty strict antijuicing[11] rules? Because CC's performance was most definitely enhanced during showcase season.

AP and JR are the perfect couple in love for three years straight. Except for that intimate time A had over the summer with TF at his beach house. Even more awkward now that the guys are friends. Think they compare notes?

I can't breathe. It's out there for everyone to see. How? Simon's dead; he can't have published this. Has someone else taken over for him? But it doesn't even matter: the how, the why, the when – all that matters is that it is. Jake will see it, if he hasn't already. All the things I read before I got to my initials, that shocked me as I realized who they were about and what they meant, fall out of my head. Nothing exists except my stupid, horrible mistake with TJ Forrester in black and white on the screen for the whole world to read.

Jake will *know*. And he'll never forgive me.

From: Karen M. McManus, *One of us is lying*, 2017 (abridged and adapted)

8 peanut ['piːnʌt] type of nut that many people are allergic to ○ **9** southpaw ['saʊθpɔː] *here:* left-handed pitcher in baseball ○ **10** to make a splash [ˌmeɪk‿ə 'splæʃ] to quickly become very successful ○ **11** antijuicing [ˌænti 'dʒuːsɪŋ] against the use of steroids

READING
12 Understanding the story
→ SB 62/7; S1, S2

a) *Sum up what happens in the novel extract. Include important information about Bronwyn, Simon, Mr Avery and Addy and describe the way that About That works.*

b) *Are the statements true or false? Tick ✔ the correct answer. In your exercise book, give evidence for the true ones and correct the false ones.*

	true	false
1. The gossip that Simon spreads on his app can be very harmful.	☐	☐
2. Mr Avery only catches a few of his students who bring phones to class.	☐	☐
3. Teachers could ban About That if they wanted to.	☐	☐
4. Bronwyn is unsure of Mr Avery's real opinions about technology and education.	☐	☐
5. It is clear that Addy is not used to writing using traditional methods.	☐	☐
6. The police have been able to get into Simon's About That account.	☐	☐
7. Addy thinks she knows who really produces the content for About That.	☐	☐
8. Addy is worried that all of her friends may see the post about her.	☐	☐

WRITING
13 Analysis: Narrative perspective and characters
→ SB 62/7; S4, S6, S7

a) *Make notes about Addy's and Bronwyn's characters. What do you find out about each of them in the first part, what do you find out in the second part? What's the difference?*

b) *Analyse the narrative perspective in the extract. Describe its effect on the reader.*

c) *Compare and contrast the information that is given about the characters' relationships with and attitudes to (1) technology and (2) About That.*

Word bank

first-person narrator | protagonist | characteristics | thoughts | emotions / feelings | use of humour | to be told about | to feel close to / distant from sb | to relate to | to identify with | from the point of view of | to see sth from sb's perspective

14 Options
→ SB 62/7; S17, S32

*Choose **one** of the following tasks.*

WRITING

a) *Write and role-play a conversation between Addy and her best friend that happens after the end of the extract. Think about how Addy feels, why she feels that way and what advice the friend gives her.*

b) *Write an outline of how the story could continue. Think about the effect of the latest post on About That on Addy, Bronwyn, Nate and Cooper. Who do you think manages the account now? What will happen once everybody has read the post?*

SPEAKING MK

c) *Discuss whether you would like to have your own About That app at your school. Give reasons.*

15 Teamwork vocabulary

→ SB 63/1

a) *Match the words to make phrases related to collaboration. Use your exercise book.*

to accept | to ask for | to assess | to assign | to check | to complete | to divide | to give | to make | to plan | to reach | to stick to | to take	a | the	decision | feedback | help | milestone | progress | responsibility | roles | schedule | task | work

b) *Write down an example sentence for each phrase from a) in your exercise book.*

A14

16 Working as a team

→ SB 63/2; S29, S31, S36

a) *Listen to what four people have to say about teamwork. Match the speakers with the aspect of teamwork they talk about. There is* ***one*** *aspect you don't need.*

1. Video game developer
2. Band member
3. TV director
4. Football coach

a) accepting feedback
b) working as a team
c) sticking to the schedule
d) assigning roles
e) sticking to one's roles

b) *Listen again. Take notes on each speaker's perspective on teamwork.*

1. Video game developer: ______________________________

____

2. Band member: ______________________________

____

3. TV director: ______________________________

____

4. Football coach: ______________________________

____

MK

c) *Discuss the speakers' perspectives in small groups. Who do you agree / disagree with? Why? Have you had similar experiences? What kind of problems have you had with teamwork?*

d) *To improve your next experience of working as a team, discuss ways to avoid the problems you talked about in c). Say why it is better to avoid these problems in the future.*

Green Line 6 G9

Workbook

Grammar, Word banks and Portfolio

〈G1〉 Revision: Adverbial clauses of time, reason, concession, contrast, comparison, place and direction

An adverbial clause is a subordinate clause which is connected to the main clause by a conjunction (often called 'linking word'). You use an adverbial clause to add information to what is said in the main clause. Adverbial clauses help you to create longer sentences and make your text flow better. There are adverbial clauses of time, reason, comparison, concession or contrast and place or direction:

time: after, as (*als*), as soon as, before, since (*seit, seitdem*), until / till, when, whenever, while (*während*)	Kim was looking online for clothes with a low ecological footprint **when** she found an interesting article about the environmental impact of the production of T-shirts.
reason: as (*da, weil*), because, since (*da, weil*)	Nowadays people buy more environmentally friendly clothes **because** they are more easily available in shops or online stores. **As** there are special labels for them, they can also be identified more easily.
comparison: than	She knows that workers in the textile industry in Bangladesh or India have to work longer hours **than** workers in England, for example.
concession or contrast: although, (even) though, whereas, while (*obwohl*)	People buy environmentally friendly clothes **even though** they are sometimes slightly more expensive. **While** customers are paying more money, many people who produce these clothes still have poor working conditions.
place or direction: everywhere, where, wherever	**Everywhere** Kim goes, she discovers products that are claimed to be environmentally friendly. She often doesn't know **where** she can find reliable information on products.

! You can often place the adverbial clause before or after the main clause. If the adverbial clause comes first, you need to put a comma between the adverbial clause and the main clause, e.g. **While** Kim was looking online for clothes with a low ecological footprint, she noticed an interesting article about the environmental impact of the production of T-shirts.

G2 Adverbial clauses of purpose and manner

You already know various types of adverbial clauses (→ G1). Two more types are adverbial clauses of purpose and manner. While you use an adverbial clause of **purpose** to describe **why** something is happening in the main clause, you use an adverbial clause of **manner** to describe **how** something is happening.

purpose: so, so that, in order to, in case	What can you do with your clothes and other products **so that** they have a longer life cycle? A lot of farmers use pesticides **in order to** make their cotton fields more profitable.
manner: like, as (*wie*), as if, as though, just as	Many people treat clothes **as though** they are disposable. According to some sources, it looks **as if** at least one-fifth of clothing in the US is never actually worn. Studies found that the last two stages in the life cycle of a T-shirt also have a large ecological footprint **just as** environmentalists had expected.

⟨G3⟩ Revision: Modals and their substitute forms

Can, can't, must, mustn't, needn't and **may** are the most common **modals**. You use them to add additional meaning to the main verb (= infinitive without to) of a sentence, i.e. ability *(Fähigkeit)*, obligation *(Verpflichtung)*, permission *(Erlaubnis)* or possibility *(Möglichkeit)*. Modals are usually used in the present tense and for all other tenses you need a substitute form. (Note: You can also use the substitute forms in the present tense.)

modal	substitute form	example
(in)ability		
can ↔ cannot / can't *(können ↔ nicht können)*	to be able to	Kim **is able to** reduce her ecological footprint by buying local produce regularly. Her family **weren't able to** find locally grown pears, so they bought apples instead. They **will be able to** buy their food from a zero-waste shop when it opens next month.
(no) obligation		
must ↔ needn't *(müssen ↔ nicht brauchen)*	to have to	Companies **have to** do more to reduce their carbon emissions. He **had to** take his phone to the repair café. They **won't have to** use their car. It's not that far so they can walk.
(no) permission, possibility		
can, could, may ↔ cannot / can't, may not, mustn't *(könnte/n; dürfen ↔ nicht dürfen)*	to be allowed to	Kim **is allowed to** use her dad's car when he doesn't need it himself. In previous years they **weren't allowed to** use the computer room without a teacher. The inhabitants of the town **won't be allowed to** drive their cars on Sundays any longer.

❗ There are two meanings of **could**:
- You use **could** as the simple past form of **can** to express an ability, e.g.
  Kim **could** reduce her ecological footprint by buying local produce.
  (= was able to reduce)
  Her family **couldn't** find locally grown pears, so they bought apples instead.
  (= wasn't able to find)
- You use **could** instead of **may I / we** in polite questions, e.g.
  Could I have three apples, please? (= May I …?)

❗ There is a slight difference in meaning between **must** and **to have to**:
- You use **must** if the speaker thinks that an action is important, e.g.
  "I **must** tidy my room today."
- You use **to have to** to show that the action is important for someone else (i.e. other than the speaker), e.g.
  Daughter: I **have to** tidy my room every Saturday.
  (because my mum told me to – action is important to her mother, not her)

G4 More modals

You already know various modals and their meanings (→ G3). Here are some more:

a) **should and ought to *(sollen)***

	modal	example
To ask for instruction or advice you use …	shall (I / we) should	**Shall** we **have** lasagne tonight? What **shall** I **cook** for dinner? What **should** he / she / they **do**?
To express an obligation you use …	should	I **should work** on my presentation after dinner.
To express advice, an opinion / criticism or an expectation for the future you use …	should ought to	I think we **should / ought to do** more to protect the environment. That **shouldn't / ought not to be** difficult to arrange.

❗ **Shall / shan't (= shall not)** is sometimes used for talking about the future instead of 'I / we will' or 'I / we won't'. However, it sounds very formal, e.g.
I **shan't** be able to attend the meeting.
We **shall** inform you of our decision next week.

In the past **shall** and **shan't** were more widely used. You can still find them in books (e.g. in novels dating back to the 18th and 19th centuries), expressions, sayings, quotations and legal English, e.g.
Somebody who **shall** remain nameless …
As you sow, so **shall** you reap.
The vendor **shall** supply documentary evidence of …

b) **might and might not *(vielleicht, eventuell, möglicherweise, unter Umständen)***
You use **might** and **might not** (= **mightn't**) …

	example
– to express a slight possibility in the future.	After my A-levels I **might spend** a year working abroad. The government **might introduce** stricter laws later on this year.
– to ask for permission (formal, not used very often).	**Might** I **ask** you for your phone number? – Yes. It's 0123 4567889.
– to express advice or to make a polite and less direct suggestion.	Server: You **might like** to try our meal of the day. (instead of: Would you like to try …?)

❗ **Might** is also used as the past form of **may** in indirect speech, e.g.
"That **may be** a problem," said Nora. → Nora said that it **might be** a problem.

❗ Often **might have + past participle** is used to express disapproval or criticism of an action in the past, e.g. You **might have told** me you were going to be late.

c) would and would not *(würden)*

You use **would** and **would not** (= **wouldn't**) …

	example
– to express a polite and formal request.	**Would** you **make** me a couple of sandwiches for lunch? (instead of: Will you make …?)
– to express an imagined situation in a conditional sentence type 2.	If we went to London by plane, we **would produce** a lot of carbon emissions.
– to express frequent actions in the past (often used in stories).	When I was young, we **would travel** to Scotland by car every summer. When my grandfather was a child, he **would help** his dad on the farm almost every day.
– to add emphasis or in a formal context.	My parents **would not approve** of the kind of stunts that some activists do. (instead of: My parents don't …)
– to talk about the future in the past.	I thought it **would rain**, so I brought my umbrella.

❗ **Would** is also used as the past form of **will** in indirect speech:
"That **will be** a problem," said Joanna. → Joanna said that it **would be** a problem.
"I'**ll pay** for the ice cream," said Jack. → He said that he **would pay** for the ice cream.

❗ To make statements sound less direct you can also use **would** with verbs such as …

to advise	I'**d advise** you to use public transport more often.
to imagine	I've never tried to be vegetarian, but I'**d imagine** it's difficult to stop eating meat.
to recommend	I'**d recommend** that you correct and rewrite the letter. (formal)
to say	I'**d say** there is a lot more we can do to save electricity.
to suggest	We'**d suggest** that you take this route. It's much shorter. (formal)
to think	I've heard that restaurant is really popular. I'**d think** you would need to call ahead and book a table.

d) used to *(früher, damals)*

You use **used to / didn't use to + infinitive** to talk about …

	example
– an action in the past that no longer happens now or a state / situation in the past that is no longer true.	Emma **used to buy** new T-shirts every month when she was younger. They **didn't use to have** good working conditions.

❗ **Used to** can only be used in the simple past, e.g.
Emma **used to buy** new T-shirts every month when she was younger.
= Emma **bought** new T-shirts every month when she was younger.

⟨G5⟩ Revision: Adjectives and adverbs

You use adjectives to give more information about a noun or pronoun, i.e. adjectives tell the readers or listeners what people or things are like. You use adverbs to refer to a verb, i.e. adverbs describe how you do something or how something happens.

adjective	adverb
The muesli bar has a great taste but comes at a small price.	The bar fits **comfortably** in your pocket.
It is healthy.	You should chew the bar **slowly** to enjoy its taste.

! You also use adjectives after …

	example
– verbs describing the state or quality of a noun: to be, to keep, to remain, to seem, to stay.	A power bank can **be** useful.
– verbs referring to a future state *(werden)*: to become, to get, to go, to grow, to turn.	By using our electric toothbrush, your teeth will **turn** white again.
– verbs of perception: to feel, to look, to smell, to sound, to taste.	The orange juice **smells** delicious.
– certain verbs used with an object + adjective: to call, to find, to keep, to like, to make, to see.	This toothpaste will **keep** your breath fresh all day.

a) Comparison of adjectives

	adjective	comparative	superlative	spelling rule
	adjectives of one syllable or adjectives of two syllables ending in -y			
comparison with -er / -est	small	smaller	the smallest	
	big	bigger	the biggest	end consonant doubles after a short vowel
	nice	nicer	the nicest	no silent -e
	easy	easier	the easiest	-y turns to i if the adjective ends with a consonant + -y (except: shy)
	healthy	healthier	the healthiest	
	adjectives of two or more syllables			
comparison with more / most	attractive	more attractive	the most attractive	
	delicious	more delicious	the most delicious	
	useful	more useful	the most useful	

! With **adjectives of two syllables ending in -le, -ow** or **-er** and some others (quiet, polite, stupid etc.) two forms are possible:
clever → cleverer / the cleverest; more clever / the most clever
gentle → gentler / the gentlest; more gentle / the most gentle
narrow → narrower / the narrowest; more narrow / the most narrow
polite → politer / the politest; more polite / the most polite

Irregular forms:
bad – worse – the worst | good – better – the best |
far – further / the farther – furthest / the farthest

- You use the **comparative** form to describe the results of change or how something is in the process of changing, e.g.
  Your teeth will be **whiter** (than before).
  Batteries are getting **more efficient**.
- You use the **superlative** form to show that one thing or person in a group has got more or less of a quality than all the others in the same group, e.g.
  Compared to going by car and flying, walking has the **lowest** carbon emissions.
- You use the phrase **as + adjective + as** to express that people, animals or things are the same with regard to a particular quality, e.g.
  The expensive toothbrush is **as good as** the cheap toothbrush.
- You use the phrase **not as + adjective + as** or **comparative + than** to express that people, animals or things aren't the same with regard to a particular quality, e.g.
  A tomato is**n't as sweet as** an apple.
  An apple is **sweeter than** a tomato.

Don't mix up **than** *(als)*, **then** *(dann)* and **when** *(als, wann)*, e.g.
It was much more expensive **than** I had expected.
He bought a new T-shirt, **then** another and **then** another.
I loved watching commercials **when** I was a kid.
Call me **when** you've finished.

b) **How to make an adverb**
To make an adverb you use the adjective + **-ly** or **-ally**:

– adjective + -ly:	Some storylines in commercials aren't understood **easily**.
– adjective ending in -ic + -ally:	Some films end **dramatically**.

Spelling rule:
adjectives ending in -y: angr**y** → angr**i**ly. happ**y** → happ**i**ly; except for: shy → shyly
adjectives ending in -le: comfortabl**e** → comfortably; terribl**e** → terribly

Good or well:
Good is an adjective and **well** is the **adverb**, e.g.
– This storyline is good.
– It was written **well**.
Well can also be used as an adjective to talk about health, e.g.
If you don't feel well, try to eat more fruit and vegetables.

Some adjectives and adverbs have **the same form**:
fast → fast, e.g. a **fast** runner; to run **fast**
early → early, e.g. an **early** night; to get up **early**
late → late, e.g. a late **night**; to get up **late**

Two different adverb forms:
hard → hard *(schwer, schwierig)* / hardly *(kaum)*, e.g. to work **hard**; he **hardly** works
late → late *(spät)* / lately *(in letzter Zeit)*, e.g. to arrive **late**; I haven't been to London **lately**

c) **Comparison of adverbs**

	adverb	comparative	superlative
	adverbs that have the same form as the adjective		
comparison with -er/-est	(to drive) fast	fast**er**	(the) fast**est**
	(to sleep) late	lat**er**	(the) lat**est**
	(to jump) high	high**er**	(the) high**est**
	(to work) hard	hard**er**	(the) hard**est**
	(to fly) low	low**er**	(the) low**est**
	adverbs ending in -y or -ally		
comparison with more/ most	(to change) quickly	**more** quickly	(the) **most** quickly
	(to come) easily	**more** easily	(the) **most** easily
	(to talk) quietly	**more** quietly	(the) **most** quietly
	(to end) dramatically	**more** dramatically	(the) **most** dramatically

! **Irregular forms:**
(to drive) badly – worse – (the) worst
(to get up) early – earlier – (the) earliest
(to go) far – further / farther – (the) furthest / farthest
(to drink) little – less – (the) least
(to eat) much – more – (the) most
(to swim) well – better – (the) best

- To show similarity, you use **as + adverb + as**, e.g.
  The electric car works **as well as** a traditional car.

- To show difference, you use **not as + adverb + as** or the **comparative + than**, e.g.
  The engine is**n't** running **as quietly as** it should.
  Our new model goes from 0 to 100 **faster than / more quickly than** other models.

〈G6〉 Revision: Tenses referring to the future

a) **The will future**

You use the **will future** (will + infinitive) …

	example
– to say that something is certain to happen in the future. The speaker cannot influence these states or events, e.g. the weather.	The students are going to be homeschooled tomorrow as the Southwest of Britain **will see** severe storms.
– to express that you think something might happen. Often with: verbs like to hope, to expect, to be sure and adverbs like probably, perhaps, possibly	I'm sure the school **will buy** some new equipment before the start of the new term. Our teachers **will** probably **get** some training on how to use this equipment in the classroom.
– for spontaneous decisions, promises and general predictions.	I'**ll call** you later today to talk about the school dance.
– to ask for help or to offer help without having planned to do this before.	**Will** you **have** a look at my phone, please? It doesn't seem to be working. – OK, I'**ll help** you in a minute. / I'**ll have** a look at it in a minute.

b) **The going-to future**

You use the **going-to future** (am / is / are + going to + infinitive) …

	example
– to talk about future plans and intentions of the speaker, listener or writer.	**I'm going to study** Computer Science.
– to talk about a strong possibility of an event happening in the future. There are clear signs that indicate this.	Due to a technical problem, there **isn't going to be** any connection to the internet today.

c) **The simple present**

You use the **simple present** (infinitive; third person singular infinitive + -es / -s) …

	example
– to talk about events that are officially fixed, e.g. in timetables, programmes and schedules. Often with: verbs like to arrive, to begin, to depart, to leave, to start, to end	The first lesson **starts** at 8:00. The lunch break **begins** at 12:30 and **ends** at 1:15. I've just checked and the 6:30 train from London **doesn't arrive** in Coventry until 7:50.

d) **The present progressive**

You use the **present progressive** (am / is / are + present participle) …

	example
– to talk about (personal) arrangements you have made for the future. Often with: verbs of movement and time phrases like tomorrow, this weekend, on Saturday, next week	We**'re meeting** at 3:30 p.m. tomorrow to carry on with our project.

G7 The will-future perfect

You use the **will-future perfect** (will have + past participle) …

	example
– to express that an action or event will have been completed at a given point in the future. Often with: by tomorrow, by then, by 2060, by the time, in 50 years' time, when my parents come back	The trial programme to test our new approach to learning **will have finished** by the end of the year.

G8 The will-future progressive

You use the **will-future progressive** (will be + present participle) …

	example
– to describe an action in progress at a certain time in the future. Often with: this time next week / month / year, over the coming days / weeks / months / years	Over the coming months, we **will be developing** an exciting VR-based collaborative learning programme.
– to describe a future action that overlaps with a shorter action or time.	When we open the first school of this type in September, we **will be offering** a more personalised approach to education.
– to say that something will happen repeatedly in the future.	Students **will be rehearsing** for the school play on Tuesday afternoons from the beginning of October.

⟨G9⟩ Revision: Relative clauses

a) Defining relative clauses and contact clauses

You use defining relative clauses to **give necessary information**. Without this information the meaning of the main clause would be unclear. You use the relative pronoun …

	example
– **who** or **that** for people. (Note: The object form **whom** is used in formal style in BE. It is commonly used in AE.)	Rankin's goal during the photo project wasn't to blame the people **who / that** had created editing apps. The people **who / that / whom** Rankin used in the project didn't usually edit their own photos.
– **which** or **that** for things or animals if not personalised.	Many teenagers use the same social media **which / that** their friends use.
– **whose** to express what belongs to somebody.	People **whose** goal is to become a well-known influencer will have to work very hard.

❗ **No comma** is used between the defining relative clause and the noun (in the main clause) it refers to.

❗ In defining relative clauses, you can leave out the **relative pronoun** if it's the object of the relative clause (i.e. the relative pronoun is followed by a **subject**), which then becomes a contact clause, e.g. The people (**who / that / whom**) **we** interviewed were all using filters.

b) Participles in place of defining relative clauses

You can replace a defining relative clause with a **participle construction**. You use …

	example
– the **present participle** to replace a defining relative clause with a verb form in the **active voice**. It can replace the simple form (a badge which states …) or the progressive form (girls who are playing …).	In a competition each player has a badge **which states** their gaming names. → … a badge **stating** their gaming names. The girls **who are playing** in the final match started doing esports at the age of 11. → The girls **playing** in the final match …

	example
– the **past participle** to replace a defining relative clause with a verb form in the **passive voice.**	I read the job description **which** **was included** in the advertisement very carefully. → I read the job description **included** in the advertisement very carefully.

c) **Non-defining relative clauses**

You use non-defining relative clauses to **add extra information** about a person or thing. This makes the sentence more interesting. But the main clause is complete and understandable without the non-defining relative clause. You use the relative pronoun …

	example
– **who** for people. (Note: The object form **whom** is used in formal style in BE. It is commonly used in AE.)	Social media influencers, **who** are mostly in their teens and twenties, can earn a lot of money. Mr Shirky, **whom** you may have seen on the internet, is an expert on the social effects of technology.
– **which** for things.	Rankin explored photo editing apps in a recent photo series, **which** is titled 'Selfie Harm.'
– **whose** to express what belongs to somebody.	The photographer, **whose** photography subjects have included celebrities, took portraits of 15 individuals wearing minimal make-up.

❗ **Never** use the relative pronoun **that** in non-defining relative clauses.

❗ **There is a comma** before the relative pronoun to separate the main clause from the relative clause. When speaking, you pause at the comma.

G10 The relative pronoun *which* to comment on the main clause

You already know the relative pronoun **which**. It can be used in defining and non-defining relative clauses to refer back to a noun in the main clause (→ G9). You can also use …

	example
You can use a **non-defining relative clause** with **which** *(was)* to comment on the main clause. It then refers to the entire main clause.	I recently tried VR for the first time, **which was an amazing experience**. Technology keeps changing, **which can make it difficult to keep up**. There are lots of free apps available, **which is good news if you don't have much money**.

❗ **There is a comma** to separate the main clause from the relative clause. When speaking, you pause at the comma.

G11 Relative clauses with *where* and *when*

You already know the relative pronouns **who, which, that** and **whose** (→ G9, G10).
Two more relative pronouns are **where** and **when**. You can use them in defining and non-defining relative clauses. If a relative clause refers …

	example
– to a place, you can use **where** instead of **in which / at which.**	That was the e-gaming camp **where** we stayed last summer. (= … **at which** we stayed last summer.) Photo editing has become an open secret in the world of social media, **where** image is everything. (= …, **in which** image is everything.)
– to a period in time, you can use **when** instead of **in which / on which / at which.**	I can't remember the date **when** the e-gaming competition starts. (= … the date **on which** the e-gaming competition starts.) Summer is the time **when** most gaming tournaments are held. (= … the time **in which** most gaming tournaments are held.)

❗ If you use expressions like **the year …, the day …** or **the time …,** you can use **when** or **that** or **leave out the relative pronoun**, e.g.
Monday is **the day (when)** we usually meet for lunch.
I can't remember **the year (that)** they moved the school to a new location.

⟨G12⟩ Revision: Tenses referring to the present

a) **The simple present**
You use the **simple present** (infinitive, third person/singular + -es/-s) …

	example
– to express **facts.**	40% of UK parents and guardians **use** location-tracking apps daily.
– to express what people **accept as true.**	Devices like computers and smartphones **don't work** without electricity.
– to talk about things that **happen regularly** or about **permanent states.** Often used with: always, often, never, regularly, sometimes, usually	A summary of a news report **is** usually 1/3 of the original text and **leaves out** details, personal opinions and interpretations.
– to describe a **series of actions or events** that happen one after another. It is often used in sports commentaries, in comments on texts and in summaries.	Tim Lewis **begins** his article by referring to a survey on apps used by parents. He **goes on** to quote an expert. In the next part he **explains** … He **concludes** the article by pointing out that …

b) **The present progressive**
You use the present progressive (am/is/are + present participle) …

	example
– to describe activities that are happening at the moment. Often used with: at the moment, just, just now, right now	The girl **is sitting** in front of the computer and **playing** a computer game. She **is wearing** headphones.
– to express gradual developments.	According to recent surveys, the number of parents who track the location of their children **is increasing**.

⟨G13⟩ Revision: Tenses referring to the past

a) Present perfect simple

You use the **present perfect simple** (has / have + past participle) …

	example
– to stress the **result of an activity or event.** The activity itself happened in the past, but the result is still relevant in the present. Often with: already, just, ever, so far, twice, three times	Leon **has taken** so many photos with his smartphone that he must save some of them to the cloud.
– for an activity or event that **began in the past and has continued until now.** Often with: for, since	He **hasn't seen** his parents for eight months.
– to express that **something hasn't happened yet** or to ask **whether something has taken place yet.** Often with: never, (not) yet	They are really excited about going to Canada because they **have never been** there before. **Have** you **paid** for the tickets yet?

❗ You use ***for*** with a **period of time** (e.g. for hours, for years, for a long time) and ***since*** with a **point in time** (e.g. since 1996, since yesterday, since she got up this morning).

❗ – **Stative verbs** (to be, to believe, to know, to see etc.) are normally used in the present perfect simple, e.g.
Leon's family **has** always **loved** active holidays.
– **Dynamic verbs** (to live, to play, to work etc.) are used in the present perfect progressive, e.g. Leon's dad **has been trying** to speak French since they arrived in Montreal.

b) The present perfect progressive

You use the **present perfect progressive** (have / has + been + present participle) …

	example
– to describe an activity which **began in the past, is still happening** in the present and **may continue** in the future. The duration and continuation of an activity are stressed.	Leon **has been enjoying** life in Toronto.
– to say how long an action has lasted. Often with: all week / day / year, since, for	Leon **has been living** in Toronto for almost eight months now. He **has been planning** things all week that he can do with his parents.
– to express that an action is repeated.	He **has been taking** kayaking lessons every second weekend this summer.

c) **The simple past**

You use the **simple past** (irregular simple past form or infinitive + -ed for regular verbs) …

	example
- to describe states, events or activities that were **completed in the past** and are now over. Often with: last week / month / year, two days / weeks / years ago, yesterday, in 2021, when	My parents and I **travelled** more than 600 miles while they were in Canada.
- to describe a series of actions or events. This makes it the basic tense in narrative texts (stories, novels) and in reports about past events.	We **spent** the first day sightseeing in Toronto and **visited** the CN Tower. On the second day …

d) **The past progressive**

You use the **past progressive** (was / were + present participle) …

	example
- to describe an activity or event that **was in progress at a certain time** in the past. It is often used to describe something that was still going on when something new happened. In this case you use the **past progressive** for the **background action** and the **simple past** for the **new action or event**. Often with: while	While I **was taking** a photo of the falls, a wave hit me.
- to talk about several activities that **were happening at the same time** in the past.	Lots of people **were watching** us while we **were doing** the Edge Walk.
- to describe **gradual developments**.	It **was getting** dark by the time Leon and his parents returned from their bike trip around Ottawa.

e) **The past perfect simple**

You use the **past perfect simple** (had + past participle) …

	example
- to describe an activity or event that **happened before another activity** or event in the past. The past perfect simple is **often used with the simple past** (active or passive). In this case the simple past describes what happened at a certain time in the past and the past perfect simple states what happened before that time. Often with: after, before, by the end of …, ever, never, still, just, (not) yet	The host family **had exchanged** emails with Leon before he **came** to stay. Leon **was shown** around on the first day at his new school after he **had met** the principal. He still **hadn't seen** all of the school by the end of his first week.

‹G14› The past perfect progressive

You use the **past perfect progressive** (had been + present participle) …

	example
– for actions that were already in progress and ended at or just before a point in the past.	Mum **had been sleeping** for some time on the plane when she was woken up by a strange noise.
– to express that an activity or event was in progress before it was interrupted by another activity or event. Often with: for, since	They **had been walking** around Toronto since 10 o'clock when they discovered a police museum.

‹G15› Revision: Indirect speech

a) Indirect speech without backshift

You use **indirect speech without backshift** to report what somebody has just said or what you have just read, e.g. to quote from a text. The **reporting verb in the introductory sentence** is in the **simple present** and **what you report is in the same tense as in direct speech**.

"My parents and I **spent** the first day sightseeing in Toronto."
→ In his blog Leon **says** in line 6 that he and his parents **spent** the first day sightseeing in Toronto.

b) Indirect speech with backshift

You use **indirect speech with backshift** to report what somebody said some time ago.
The **reporting verb in the introductory sentence** is in the **past tense** and the **tense in the reported sentences changes** (= backshift).

direct speech	indirect speech with backshift
simple present → Host dad: The job in the forest industry **is** suited to my interests.	simple past He explained to Leon (that) the job in the forest industry **was** suited to his interests.
present progressive → I'**m going** to work now.	past progressive He told his family (that) he **was going** to work then.
present perfect simple → Leon's mom: I'**ve** never **been** to Toronto before.	past perfect simple She explained that she **had** never **been** to Toronto before.
simple past → I **saw** a police officer wearing a turban.	past perfect simple She mentioned that she **had seen** a police officer wearing a turban.
past perfect simple = We **hadn't realised** French is the main language in Montreal.	past perfect simple They admitted they **hadn't realised** that French is the main language in Montreal.
can + infinitive → Host dad: You **can't visit** Montreal without trying poutine!	could + infinitive He told us we **couldn't** visit Montreal without trying poutine.
will + infinitive → Leon: I'**ll send** you some photos from Niagara Falls.	would + infinitive Leon said he **would send** his host family some photos from Niagara Falls.

❗ Remember to change **pronouns** and **possessive determiners**, e.g.
Leon: **I** have just checked **my** emails. → He said **he** had just checked **his** emails.

❗ When using indirect speech with backshift, remember to change **phrases of time and place** if things are reported on another day or if people are in different places. You may also need to change the **verbs** to come (→ to go) and to bring (→ to take), e.g.

Richard: I don't have time to help you **now**.
Richard said he didn't have time to help me **then**.
Sally: I couldn't wait to **come here**.
Sally said she couldn't wait to **go there**.

now → then
today → that day
this evening → that evening
yesterday → the day before
two weeks ago → two weeks before
tomorrow → the next day
last year → the previous year, the year before
here → there

❗ **Questions in indirect speech:**

- For **questions with a question word**, use **asked** or **wanted to know + question word,** e.g.
  Taxi driver: **Where** do you want to go?
  → The taxi driver asked **where** the passenger wanted to go.
- For **questions without a question word**, use **if**, e.g.
  Taxi driver: Will you stay in Toronto for long?
  → The taxi driver wanted to know **if** the passenger would stay in Toronto for long.

❗ **Requests and commands in indirect speech:**

- Use **tell sb to do sth** for commands and **ask sb to do sth** for requests, e.g.
  Friend: Don't get your hopes up too high, Leon.
  → A friend **told** Leon **not to get** his hopes up too high.
  Host mum: Please be polite to Leon.
  → The host mum **asked** her daughter **to be** polite to Leon.

〈G16〉 Expressing probability

You use **to be supposed to, to be likely to, to be said to, to be certain to** and **to happen to + infinitive** to express chances of probability. The emphasis is on the activity that is expected to happen and not on the chances of something happening. The speaker / writer may or may not be able to prove that the event in question is true.

to be supposed to	= to be generally believed or expected to be/do sth
	The resort town of Whistler **is supposed to be** environmentally friendly. *Der Ferienort Whistler **gilt als** umweltfreundlich.*
to be likely to	= very probably
	In just one generation, the glacier **is likely to disappear**. *Innerhalb nur einer Generation wird der Gletscher **wahrscheinlich** verschwunden sein.*
to be said to	= They say …; to be believed to be / do sth
	The chemicals **are said to endanger** and **pollute** nearby rivers. *Die Chemikalien **sollen** die nahe gelegenen Flüsse gefährden und verschmutzen./**Man sagt, dass** die Chemikalien …*
to be certain to	= sth that you can rely on to happen or to be true
	Environmentalists believe that the experience **is certain to change** the behaviour and lifestyle of the visitors. *Umweltschützende sind der Meinung, dass diese Erfahrung **sehr wahrscheinlich/mit hoher Wahrscheinlichkeit** das Verhalten und den Lebensstil der Besuchenden ändern wird.*

to happen to	= (to do or be something) by chance
	The areas where fracking is done also **happen to have** a higher risk of earthquakes. *In den Gebieten, in denen Fracking betrieben wird, besteht **zufällig/ zufälligerweise** auch ein höheres Risiko für Erdbeben.*

⟨G17⟩ Revision: The passive

You use the active voice to stress what the subject does, but the **passive voice** to **stress what is done**. You form the passive voice using **a form of to be + past participle** (irregular form or infinitive + ed).

tense	form of to be + past participle	example
simple present	am / is / are + past participle	The play **is directed** by a new director.
simple past	was / were + past participle	The music **was composed** by Andrew Lloyd Webber.
present perfect simple	have / has been + past participle	Flyers **have been printed** and need to be distributed.
past perfect simple	had been + past participle	The show **had been sold out** long before the premiere.
going-to future	am / is / are going to be + past participle	Rehearsals **are going to be held** in the assembly hall on Tuesday afternoons.
will future	will be + past participle	Lots of VIPs **will be invited** to the show.

When changing an active sentence into a passive one, the **object of the active sentence becomes the subject of the passive sentence.** The subject of the active sentence is often left out when it isn't important to say who causes the action. However, if you need to include the person who causes the action in order to make the passive sentence clearer or easier to understand, you use 'by'.

Active voice: **Andrew Lloyd Webber** composed the music.
Passive voice: The music was composed **by Andrew Lloyd Webber**.

! News headlines often use the past participle only, e.g. 'New London theatre **opened**' instead of 'New London theatre **was opened**'.

⟨G18⟩ Revision: Conditional sentences

There are three basic types of conditional sentences. They all have two parts: an if-clause and a main clause. The if-clause expresses a condition and the main clause describes a consequence.

a) **Realistic condition: The condition may be fulfilled in the future.**

	example
You use type 1 sentences for actions that are probable / possible. The verb in the if-clause is in the **simple present**; the verb in the main clause is in the **will future**, a **modal verb + infinitive** or an **imperative**.	If you give the wrong answer to a CAPTCHA, the system **will generate** a new one and ask you to try again. If you need help, you **can call** the help desk or **look for** FAQs or tutorials online. If the help desk line is busy, **try** again later.

b) **Theoretical condition: The condition is unlikely to be fulfilled in the future; it is purely theoretical.**

	example
You use type 2 sentences for actions that are (currently) hypothetical. The verb in the if-clause is in the **simple past**; the verb in the main clause is in the **conditional tense** (= would / could / might + infinitive).	Maybe it **would help** if I **understood** how the bees got in your house. You **would get** a better reaction if you **were** more polite.

c) **Condition no longer possible: The condition can no longer be fulfilled because it refers to a situation in the past which is over now.**

	example
You use type 3 sentences to say that the condition can no longer be fulfilled because it refers to a situation in the past. The verb in the if-clause is in the **past perfect simple**; the verb in the main clause is in the **conditional perfect** (would / could / might have + past participle).	I **wouldn't have called** the help desk if I **hadn't needed** advice from an expert. You **could have saved** some time if you **had called** earlier and asked for help.

! If the if-clause comes first, you need to put a **comma** between the if-clause and the main clause.

! **When** or **if**:

when	– meaning 'as soon as' / *sobald* – time matters – something is sure to happen	**When** I see my cousin tomorrow, I'll tell him about my computer problems. ***Sobald*** *ich meinen Cousin morgen sehe, werde ich ihm von meinen Computerproblemen erzählen.*
if	– meaning *falls* – the condition matters – it's not sure whether something will happen	**If** I see my cousin tomorrow, I'll tell him about my computer problems. ***Falls*** *ich meinen Cousin morgen sehe, werde ich ihm von meinen Computerproblemen erzählen.*

Reducing your ecological footprint

food

to write a shopping list
to go to the local farmer's market
to eat less meat
to start composting
to buy fresh and local food

consumption

to buy fair trade
to buy second-hand
to regift
to repair broken / torn things
to swap clothes
to share
to upcycle
to use recycled paper

plastic

to avoid plastic packaging
to bring your own bags
to use a glass or steel container as lunchbox
to use a reusable water bottle
to use biodegradable materials
to wear natural fabrics

What can I do?

transportation

to use public transport
to drive less
to carpool
to cycle

home

to choose energy efficient devices
to turn off devices when you don't use them
to let clothes dry outside
to use LED light bulbs
to switch to green power

activism

to be on a student council
to do a beach clean-up
to do a stunt to get attention
to get involved in an NGO (non-governmental organisation)
to learn more about climate change
to persuade friends to become active
to plant trees
to protest
to sign petitions
to take part in a protest movement
to vote in elections

Word bank

The ABSs of activism

A activist

B banner

C council

D digital activism

E equality

F fundraiser

G global warming

H human rights

I impact

J justice

K keep trying

L laws

M movement

N non-violent

O organised

P petition

Q quit flying

R research information online

S strike

T teach others

U unsatisfied citizens

V volunteer

W women's rights

X xenophobia

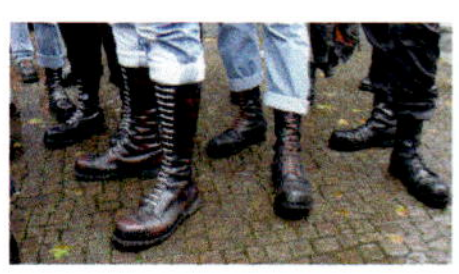

Y youth activism

Z zero waste

Our digital lives

Digital realities

AR goggles
augmented reality (AR)
avatar
computer-generated
to enhance
hybrid
to immerse in / immersive / immersion
to interact with / interactive / interaction
metaverse
virtual reality (VR)
VR headset
three-dimensional (3D)
virtual / virtually

Digital education

to adapt
approach
to collaborate / collaborative
curriculum
to develop
digital environment
education
to enroll / enrolment
gamification
to individualise
innovative / innovation
learning platform
to motivate / motivation / motivating
to personalise
skill
trial-and-error learning

Social media

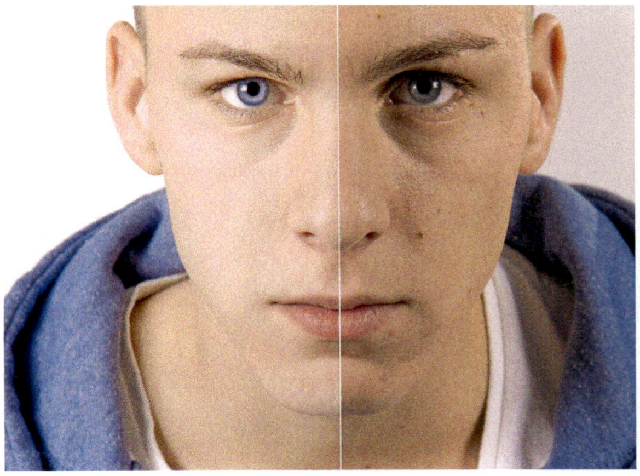

to alter / altered
appearance
comments
content
cyberbully / cyberbullying
device
to edit
editing app
fake
filter
ideal
image
influencer
to label
to post
to retouch
social media
realistic / unrealistic

Gaming

account
character
to communicate / communication
to compete / competition / competitive
console
controller
esports
game developer
to game / gamer / (online) gaming
headset
graphics
keyboard
to play
screen
user
username

Structuring argumentatives text

Introduction
- Today, you can see … everywhere.
- Obviously, most people …
- The question of the essay is whether …
- In this text, I would like to address …
- The issue focused on is …
- My goal is to …
- As the following arguments will show, …

(Counter) Arguments / Pros and cons
- First (of all), …
- The main reason is …
- Second / Third / Next, …
- However / Nevertheless, …
- On the one hand …, on the other hand …
- As a result, / Therefore …
- Although it is true that …, it would be wrong to claim that …
- Some might say … / One could argue that …
- (But) I am convinced that …
- Furthermore / Additionally / In addition, …
- Moreover / Also, …
- Another aspect / point is that …

Quotations / Facts
- The numbers show …
- According to …,
- An important fact is …
- Therefore …
- As … have / has often said, …
- It is a fact that …
- For several reasons, it is necessary …
- There are many / various reasons for this.
- Another significant point is …
- Because of … / That is why …
- For example / instance, … / Look at …

Conclusion
- To sum up … / In conclusion, …
- In summary, it can be said that …
- In my opinion, …
- My suggestion would be …
- After all, …
- Weighing the pros and cons, I conclude / come to the conclusion that …
- All in all I believe that …

Analysing graphic novels

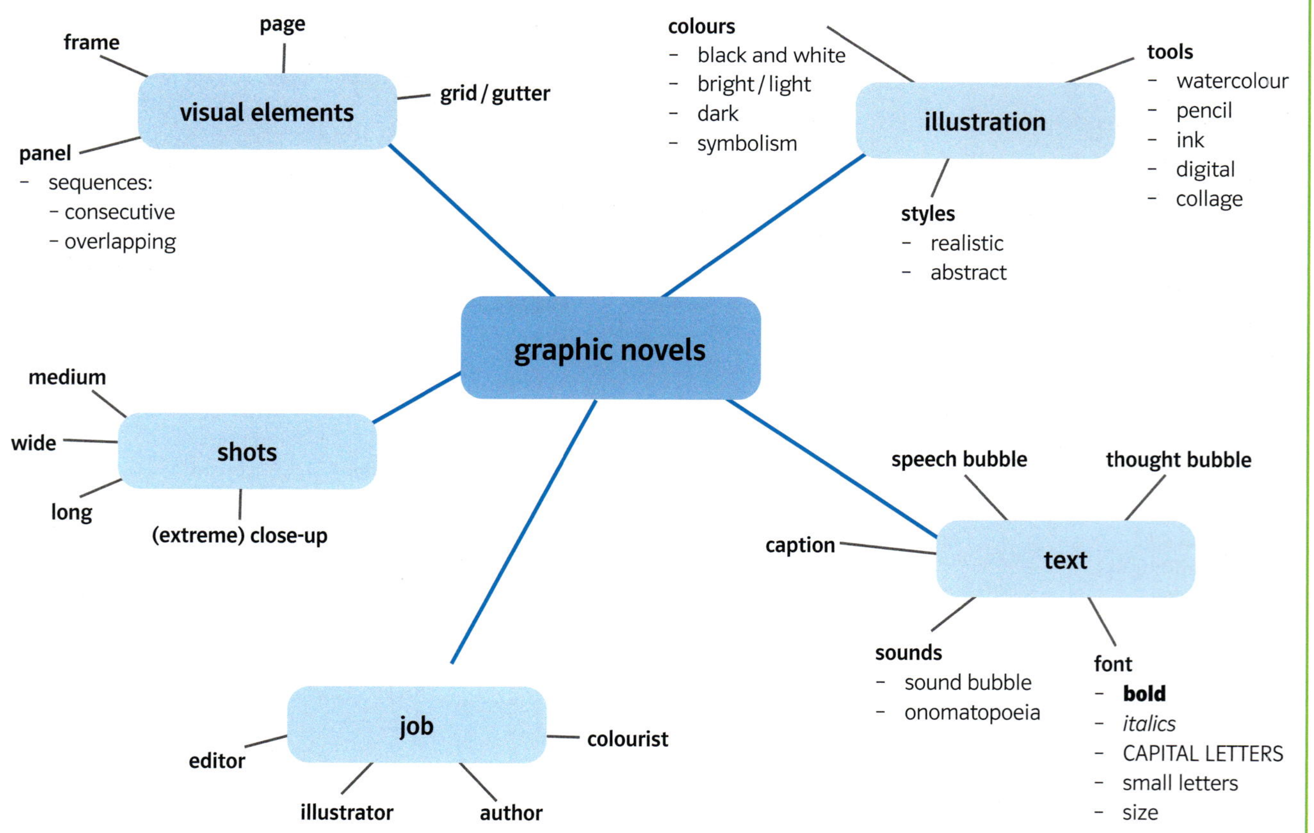

Describing a country

Landscapes

woods / forest

meadow

farmland

desert

mountains

swamp

cliff

bay

Natural resources and population

coal

timber

copper

gold

natural gas

oil

to pump up gas / oil

renewable energies

densely populated

sparsely populated

to be two times bigger / smaller than
population growth
to emigrate ⟶ emigrant
to immigrate ⟶ immigrant
to be born in

Talking about environmental issues

Causes
increase in greenhouse gases
exploiting resources
deforestation
destruction of ecosystems
population increase
using fossil fuels
water / air pollution

Effects
global warming
rising temperature
rising sea level
higher ocean temperature
increase in heavier rain
melting glaciers / permafrost
heat risks
extinction / migration of species

Modul 1

Texte und Übungen

Text ______________________________ hat mir gefallen, weil er ...

☐ spannend war ☐ interessant war ☐ meinen Hobbys / Interessen entsprach

☐ leicht verständlich war ☐ gut strukturiert war ☐ ______________

Text ______________________________ hat mir nicht so gefallen, weil ...

____

____

Diese Übung(en) ______________________________ ist / sind mir schwer gefallen, weil ich ...

☐ die Arbeitsanweisung nicht richtig verstanden habe

☐ Probleme hatte, den Wortschatz zu verstehen

☐ die Grammatikregel(n) nicht richtig verstanden habe

☐ ______________________________

Unit task

Das ist mir während der Unit task leicht gefallen: ______________________________

Das ist mir während der Unit task schwer gefallen: ______________________________

Meine Gruppe ...

☐ hat konzentriert gearbeitet ☐ hat die meiste Zeit Englisch gesprochen ☐ war kreativ

☐ ______________________________

Die Mitglieder der Gruppe ...

☐ haben die Aufgaben gerecht verteilt ☐ haben einander zugehört ☐ waren höflich zueinander

☐ ______________________________

Nächstes Mal könnten wir Folgendes besser/anders machen:

____

____

Das kann ich schon!

Hier kannst du feststellen, was du schon alles kannst oder noch üben musst. Schau dir die Aufgaben auf den Seiten im Workbook noch einmal an. Welches Ampellicht hast du bei den in der Tabelle unten angeführten Lernzielen und Übungen jeweils ausgemalt? Trage dein Ergebnis in die Tabelle ein, indem du die Ampellichter ausmalst. Die letzte Spalte zeigt dir an, wo du in deinem Buch Übungen zum Wiederholen findest, z. B. SB 15/3 → im Schulbuch auf Seite 15, Übung 3.

Ich kann	Übung(en)	Auswertung	Wiederholung
VOCABULARY			
• andere Wortarten einer Wortfamilie bilden	1 a)	○ ○ ○	Vocabulary Check-in; S2
• mit Wortschatz zu den Themen Konsum, Verbraucherschutz und Umweltschutz/ Nachhaltigkeit umgehen	1 b), 2, 9, 13	○ ○ ○	SB 15/3, SB 17/2–3, SB 21/1–2, SB 23/1, SB 33/4
LISTENING			
• einem Radiointerview wesentliche Informationen entnehmen	3	○ ○ ○	SB 15/3, SB 17/2c); S29
• persönlichen Kommentaren wesentliche und detaillierte Informationen entnehmen	7	○ ○ ○	SB 18/6; S29
GRAMMAR			
• ⟨Wiederholung: Adverbialsätze und *linking words* richtig verwenden⟩	4	○ ○ ○	SB 17/4; ⟨G1⟩
• *adverbs of purpose and manner* richtig verwenden	5	○ ○ ○	SB 18/5–6; G2
• ⟨Wiederholung: *modals* und ihre Ersatzformen sicher verwenden⟩	10	○ ○ ○	SB 21/3; ⟨G3⟩
• die *modals* ‚shall', ‚might', ‚ought to' und ‚would' korrekt verwenden	11	○ ○ ○	SB 21/4; G4
• Formen von 'used to' richtig verwenden	12	○ ○ ○	SB 22/5–6; G4
SPEAKING			
• eine Kurzpräsentation halten	6	○ ○ ○	SB 18/5; S30
• über nachhaltigen Konsum diskutieren	7 c)	○ ○ ○	SB 18/6
WRITING			
• einen Online-Kommentar schreiben	14	○ ○ ○	SB 23/2
• einen Cartoon analysieren	15	○ ○ ○	SB 23/3; S13
• einen Romanauszug analysieren	17, 18	○ ○ ○	SB 26/5; S4, S6–7
MEDIATION			
• die wesentlichen Informationen aus einem englischsprachigen Online-Artikel ins Deutsche übertragen	8	○ ○ ○	SB 18/7; S34
READING			
• einem Romanauszug wesentliche Informationen entnehmen	16	○ ○ ○	SB 26/Text, SB 26/2; S1–2
SKILLS			
• Sprachregister und Sprachstil eines formellen Briefes verbessern	20	○ ○ ○	SB 27/1; S8, S18

Modul 2

Texte und Übungen

Text ______________________________ hat mir gefallen, weil er …

☐ spannend war ☐ interessant war ☐ meinen Hobbys / Interessen entsprach

☐ leicht verständlich war ☐ gut strukturiert war ☐ ______________

Text ______________________________ hat mir nicht so gefallen, weil …

____

____

Diese Übung(en) ______________________ ist / sind mir schwer gefallen, weil ich …

☐ die Arbeitsanweisung nicht richtig verstanden habe

☐ Probleme hatte, den Wortschatz zu verstehen

☐ die Grammatikregel(n) nicht richtig verstanden habe

☐ ______________________________

Unit task

Das ist mir während der Unit task leicht gefallen: ______________________

Das ist mir während der Unit task schwer gefallen: ______________________

Meine Gruppe …

☐ hat konzentriert gearbeitet ☐ hat die meiste Zeit Englisch gesprochen ☐ war kreativ

☐ ______________________________

Die Mitglieder der Gruppe …

☐ haben die Aufgaben gerecht verteilt ☐ haben einander zugehört ☐ waren höflich zueinander

☐ ______________________________

Nächstes Mal könnten wir Folgendes besser/anders machen:

____

____

Das kann ich schon!

Hier kannst du feststellen, was du schon alles kannst oder noch üben musst. Schau dir die Aufgaben auf den Seiten im Workbook noch einmal an. Welches Ampellicht hast du bei den in der Tabelle unten angeführten Lernzielen und Übungen jeweils ausgemalt? Trage dein Ergebnis in die Tabelle ein, indem du die Ampellichter ausmalst. Die letzte Spalte zeigt dir an, wo du in deinem Buch Übungen zum Wiederholen findest, z. B. SB 56/3 → im Schulbuch auf Seite 56, Übung 3.

Ich kann	Übung(en)	Auswertung	Wiederholung
VOCABULARY			
• mit Wortschatz zu den Themen Digitales, Soziale Medien und Filmanalyse sicher umgehen	1 a)–b), 4, 10, 11	○ ○ ○	Vocabulary Check-in, SB 56/3, SB 59/2, SB 59/3
LISTENING			
• persönlichen Aussagen wesentliche Informationen entnehmen	16	○ ○ ○	SB 63/2; S29
GRAMMAR			
• ⟨Wiederholung: Zeitformen die Zukünftiges ausdrücken sicher verwenden⟩	2	○ ○ ○	SB 53/3; ⟨G6⟩
• das *future progressive* und *future perfect* richtig bilden und verwenden	3	○ ○ ○	SB 53/4; G7–8
• ⟨Wiederholung: *defining* und *non-defining relative clauses* richtig verwenden⟩	5	○ ○ ○	SB 56/4; ⟨G9⟩
• das Relativpronomen *which* verwenden, um den Hauptsatz zu kommentieren	6	○ ○ ○	SB 56/4–5; G10
• *where*, *when* und *which* richtig verwenden	7	○ ○ ○	SB 57/7; G11
SPEAKING			
• über die eigene Mediennutzung sprechen	1 c)	○ ○ ○	SB 51/2
• ein Spiel (online / PC / Konsole) präsentieren	9	○ ○ ○	SB 58/11; S30
WRITING			
• einen Romanauszug analysieren	13	○ ○ ○	SB 62/7; S4, S6–7
MEDIATION			
• wesentliche Informationen aus einem deutschen Artikel ins Englische übertragen	8	○ ○ ○	SB 58/10; S34
READING			
• einem Romanauszug wesentliche und detaillierte Informationen entnehmen	12	○ ○ ○	SB 62/7; S1–2
SKILLS			
• als Team erfolgreich zusammenarbeiten	15, 16	○ ○ ○	SB 63/1–2

Modul 3

Texte und Übungen

Text ______________________ hat mir gefallen, weil er …

☐ spannend war ☐ interessant war ☐ meinen Hobbys / Interessen entsprach

☐ leicht verständlich war ☐ gut strukturiert war ☐ ______________

Text ______________________ hat mir nicht so gefallen, weil …

____

____

Diese Übung(en) ______________ ist / sind mir schwer gefallen, weil ich …

☐ die Arbeitsanweisung nicht richtig verstanden habe

☐ Probleme hatte, den Wortschatz zu verstehen

☐ die Grammatikregel(n) nicht richtig verstanden habe

☐ ____

Unit task

Das ist mir während der Unit task leicht gefallen: ______________

Das ist mir während der Unit task schwer gefallen: ______________

Meine Gruppe …

☐ hat konzentriert gearbeitet ☐ hat die meiste Zeit Englisch gesprochen ☐ war kreativ

☐ ____

Die Mitglieder der Gruppe …

☐ haben die Aufgaben gerecht verteilt ☐ haben einander zugehört ☐ waren höflich zueinander

☐ ____

Nächstes Mal könnten wir Folgendes besser/anders machen:

____

____

Das kann ich schon!

Hier kannst du feststellen, was du schon alles kannst oder noch üben musst. Schau dir die Aufgaben auf den Seiten im Workbook noch einmal an. Welches Ampellicht hast du bei den in der Tabelle unten angeführten Lernzielen und Übungen jeweils ausgemalt? Trage dein Ergebnis in die Tabelle ein, indem du die Ampellichter ausmalst. Die letzte Spalte zeigt dir an, wo du in deinem Buch Übungen zum Wiederholen findest, z. B. SB 86/2 → im Schulbuch auf Seite 86, Übung 2.

Ich kann	Übung(en)	Auswertung	Wiederholung
VOCABULARY			
• andere Wortarten einer Wortfamilie bilden	1	○ ○ ○	SB 86/2; S2
• *phrases* bilden	3	○ ○ ○	SB 89/1
• Wortschatz zu den Themen Arbeit, Umwelt sowie Länder und Regionen sicher verwenden	6 a), 9, 14	○ ○ ○	SB 90/6, SB 92/2, SB 93/7
LISTENING			
• einer geführten Tour Details entnehmen	2	○ ○ ○	SB 87/3; S29
• einem Bericht wesentliche Informationen und Details entnehmen	8	○ ○ ○	SB 92/1; S29
GRAMMAR			
• ⟨Wiederholung: das *past perfect progressive* richtig verwenden⟩	4	○ ○ ○	SB 89/3; ⟨G13–14⟩
• ⟨Wiederholung: Indirekte Rede mit *backshift* richtig verwenden⟩	5	○ ○ ○	SB 90/4; ⟨G13–15⟩
• ⟨Wiederholung: *expressions of probability* richtig verwenden⟩	10, 11	○ ○ ○	SB 92/3-4; ⟨G16⟩
SPEAKING			
• über Videolebensläufe diskutieren	6 b)	○ ○ ○	SB 90/6; S21
• einen Videolebenslauf drehen	6 c)	○ ○ ○	SB 90/6; S16
• über Bilder sprechen	12	○ ○ ○	SB 93/5; S11
• eine Tradition in einem Video präsentieren	15	○ ○ ○	SB 94/4; S16
WRITING			
• einen Cartoon analysieren	13	○ ○ ○	SB 93/6; S13
• einen Comicromanauszug analysieren	18	○ ○ ○	SB 119/8; S4, S11
MEDIATION			
• wesentliche Informationen aus einem englischsprachigen Text ins Deutsche übertragen	7	○ ○ ○	SB 90/7; S34
READING			
• einem Comicromanauszug wesentliche Informationen und Details entnehmen	16, 17	○ ○ ○	SB 119/8; S1–2
SKILLS			
• eine Adaption erstellen	20, 21, 22	○ ○ ○	SB 120/1–4; SB 120/ Skills box

Bildquellennachweis:

U1.1 Unsplash, Montréal, QC (Daniel Novykov); **U2.2** plainpicture GmbH & Co. KG RF, Hamburg (DEEPOL); **19.1** stock.adobe.com, Dublin (monticellllo); **19.2** ShutterStock.com RF, New York (HollyHarry); **19.3** stock.adobe.com, Dublin (contrastwerkstatt); **19.4** 123rf Germany, c/o Inmagine GmbH, Nidderau (Olena Yakobchuk); **19.5** Avenue Images GmbH, Hamburg (PhotoDisc); **19.6**Getty Images Plus, München (Halfpoint); **20.1** ShutterStock.com RF, New York (MikeDotta); **20.2** ShutterStock.com RF, New York (nicostock); **20.3** stock.adobe.com, Dublin (JackF); **20.4** ShutterStock.com RF, New York (goodluz); **20.5** Getty Images Plus, München (Photodisc/D-BASE); **20.6** stock.adobe.com, Dublin (Africa Studio); **20.7** stock.adobe.com, Dublin (Lasse Kristensen); **20.8** Getty Images, München (PATRICK HERTZOG/AFP); **20.9** ShutterStock.com RF, New York (marekuliasz); **20.10** stock.adobe.com, Dublin (gorosi); **20.11** ShutterStock.com RF, New York (Allison C Bailey); **20.12** ShutterStock.com RF, New York (wavebreakmedia); **20.13** dreamstime.com, Brentwood, TN (Ericcrama); **20.14** VISUM Foto GmbH, München (Alfred Buellesbach); **20.15** ShutterStock.com RF, New York (REDPIXEL.PL); **20.16** stock.adobe.com, Dublin (Wrangler); **20.17** ShutterStock.com RF, New York (Martin Wheeler III); **20.18** iStockphoto, Calgary, Alberta (Anna Bryukhanova); **20.19** Picture-Alliance, Frankfurt/M. (SULUPRESS.DE); **20.20** ShutterStock.com RF, New York (Monkey Business Images); **20.21** ShutterStock.com RF, New York (Aaron Amat); **20.22** Getty Images Plus, München (SDI Productions); **20.23** ShutterStock.com RF, New York (Hans Christiansson); **20.24** Action Press GmbH, Hamburg (GAUL,HANS-GEORG); **20.25** ShutterStock.com RF, New York (Michal Urbanek); **20.26** Okapia, Frankfurt (Berthold Singler); **21.1** ShutterStock.com RF, New York (Gorodenkoff); **21.2** ShutterStock.com RF, New York (LightField Studios); **21.3** ShutterStock.com RF, New York (Galovtsik Gabor); **21.4** ShutterStock.com RF, New York (Friends Stock); **23.1** Ernst Klett Verlag GmbH, Stuttgart (Bernhard Knauer); **23.2** MEV Verlag GmbH, Augsburg; **23.3** iStockphoto, Calgary, Alberta (Avalon_Studio); **23.4** MEV Verlag GmbH, Augsburg; **23.5** iStockphoto, Calgary, Alberta (Daniel Breckwoldt); **23.6** stock.adobe.com, Dublin (Aleksander Bolbot); **23.7** Getty Images Plus, München (iStock/RicoK69); **23.8** Ernst Klett Verlag GmbH, Stuttgart (J.-B. Haversath, Fürstenzell); **23.9** iStockphoto, Calgary, Alberta (dgmata); **23.10** MEV Verlag GmbH, Augsburg; **23.11** ShutterStock.com RF, New York (Kotomiti Okuma); **23.13** Thinkstock, München (farvatar); **23.14** Getty Images Plus, München (E+/alacatr); **23.15** Ingram Publishing, Tattenhall Chester; **23.16** Image Source, Köln (Imagesource); **23.17** Thinkstock, München (iStock Editorial/hehague); **23.18** 123rf Germany, c/o Inmagine GmbH, Nidderau (Ekaterina Kondratova); **23.19** ShutterStock.com RF, New York (Rich Carey); **23.20** ShutterStock.com RF, New York (Piyaset);

17 Plan how you are going to work

→ SB 64/Step 1; S36

a) *What (types of) talk shows do you know, or watch or listen to yourself? How do they compare? Think about the types of hosts and guests, the content, the purpose and register of these different shows. The photos might help you.*

b) *Discuss what type of talk show is suitable for your project. Can you use a real talk show as a model?*

18 Work on your tasks

→ SB 64/Step 4; S35, S37

Write a short profile for your role, which the host can use to prepare. You can include the following information and use the words and phrases on the right.

name | job | age | personality | interests | opinion about the topic | personal experiences | knowledge

Word bank

to be shy / outgoing / quiet / loud / biased / understanding / serious / funny | to be interested in | to (not) believe | to challenge an idea | to be an expert in / on sth | to want sb to know that

Can you ...?

Stelle mithilfe des Bewertungsbogens im Beihefter auf Seite 27 fest, was du schon kannst oder noch üben musst.

Dealing with factual texts

WRITING

1 Write a summary

→ SB 76/6; S17, S23

a) *Read the article. Make notes on the main point in each paragraph for a summary.*

Can gaming be good for you?

A traditional view of video games is that they are, at best, innocent fun and, at worst, a damaging waste of time. Parents are often concerned about the effects on child gamers, and many a family argument has centred on the amount of time children spend holding a gaming controller. However, a study published recently in the Journal of the American Medical Association (JAMA) has found that video games may actually have a positive effect on children's cognitive development.

The research collected data from almost 2,000 children aged nine and ten, and is the largest study of this type that has so far been completed. The subjects were divided into two groups: those who spent more than three hours a day gaming and those who never gamed. The researchers found that the gamers performed better in tests which assessed their short-term[1] memory and their impulse control (i.e. the ability to think before acting and to change behaviour as a result). They also found that the gamers had more activity in areas of the brain[2] connected with attention and with working memory (the ability to remember information temporarily while performing tasks). The study did not make a difference between the types of video games played, but most people would probably agree that the age group in the study prefers games that move at a fast pace like shooter and action-adventure games to slower games such as puzzles.

The obvious conclusion to be drawn from the study is that gaming can be viewed more positively by parents, as it may have significant benefits for children's cognitive development. However, other factors still suggest that gaming can be harmful for children. In 2019 the World Health Organisation recognised 'internet gaming disorder' as a mental illness, which means being unable to stop playing even though it has negative consequences on other aspects of life, such as family relationships, school, work and sleep. The three hours per day used as a reference point in the JAMA study may not be considered excessive, but it is a possible stage on the way to addiction. Despite this issue, time spent gaming is time not spent on outdoor games, constructive play, reading books and other activities which have long been viewed as essential for children's physical, mental and social development.

Because video gaming is so popular among children, people fear that this generation will show a lack of basic skills in other areas and is facing future health problems. On the other hand, improved cognitive development as a result of gaming as assessed in the JAMA study might have significant benefits later in life. As is so often the case, there are no easy answers for parents.

b) *Write your summary.*

c) *Check each other's summaries and give feedback.*

Word bank

to report on | to explain | to describe | to begin by doing sth | to refer to | to discuss | to illustrate | to quote | to go on to do sth | to conclude | to suggest | according to

Checklist: Summary

- 30–40 % of original length
- state title, author, main point, source and date (if known) in the introduction
- main part structured in paragraphs
- no personal opinion
- formal register

1 short-term [ˌʃɔ:t'tɜ:m] lasting for a short time only ○ **2** brain [breɪn] the organ inside one's head that controls all body functions

READING

2 Analysing "Can gaming be good for you?" → SB 77/8; S4

a) *Answer these questions about the article in ex. 1. Give examples and lines to support your answers. Use your exercise book.*

1. Is the article objective, or does it try to persuade the reader of something?
2. Does the article give just one side of the topic, or does it present both sides of the argument?
3. Is the article well-written, convincing and interesting?

b) *Put the paragraphs of this analysis of the article in ex. 1 into the correct order.*

☐ The writer introduces and presents the results of the research. The details about the study and the results are explained in a clear, simple way.

☐ The article is easy to follow and does not use any special scientific vocabulary. It seems to have been written for the general reader. It gives a balanced and objective view of the topic.

☐ In the article entitled "Can gaming be good for you?" the writer refers to a study which suggests that playing video games may improve children's cognitive abilities.

☐ After that, the article presents some arguments against children spending a lot of time gaming, and explains in a convincing way why the study may not prove anything.

WRITING

3 Writing an analysis → SB 77/8; S4, S17

a) *Read the article and answer the questions in ex. 2a). You can use a dictionary for help. Find examples and give lines to support your ideas. Use your exercise book.*

The rise of the child fashion influencer

Pre-school children are not known for their great interest in the latest fashions, yet an increasingly high number of fashion 'mini-influencers' can be found on the internet. These children are photographed posing in mini versions of adult fashions. They appear not as children, but as tiny adults, dressed up and posed as if they were fashion-conscious young women (almost all are girls). Along with the photos, there may be comments that look like they're coming from the child ("I just love the colours of this year's autumn styles!") and comments from viewers. Of course, the content has not been created by the children themselves (not many four-year-olds can type or buy a tiny purse, after all) but by their parents.

Why would any parent do this to their child? The answer is simple: money. A successful mini-influencer can earn up to $1 for every ten followers, and may have hundreds of thousands of them. Promoting a product can earn someone thousands of dollars. Without a doubt, managing a mini-influencer on social media can become a successful family business. So can running a café, but in that case the children would not be allowed to make the coffees. In the UK, it is illegal for children to work under the age of 13. There are exceptions for acting and modelling, but only with very strict controls. There are similar regulations in most developed nations. Mini-influencers' parents usually argue that for the child, dressing up and posing in front of a camera is just family fun. However, we can only wonder how many hours it takes to get those 'perfect' looks and those 'perfect' shots, and how much fun it really is.

A key issue here is consent, so asking for and getting permission. Can a pre-school child really give permission when they have little idea of what is actually going on? Another issue is the psychological influence of becoming famous at such an early age. A third factor is the money, and who gets it. Without proper regulations, the world of mini-influencers is looking dangerously close to child exploitation.

b) *Choose one or more aspects of the text that you want to analyse. Write an outline, then write an analysis in your exercise book.*

WRITING

4 An essay on cyberbullying → SB 80/5; S17, S25

a) *Look at the outline for an essay on whether cyberbullying can be stopped (Paragraph 1: Pros 1–2, Paragraph 2: Cons 1–2). Put the following notes in the correct places in the outline (introduction and main part). Then look at the Skills box in d) on the next page and add your own ideas for the conclusion.*

cyberbullying is a very complex behaviour | online content is difficult to control | cyberbullying: examples + definition | harsher punishment[1] for bullies | people can be educated to change their behaviour | impossible to delete harmful content completely | ask: is it possible to stop cyberbullying? | change laws to fight cyberbullying

title: "Is it possible to stop cyberbullying?"		
introduction		
– ______ – *common problem: recent German study says nearly 1/3 of teens have received harmful / offensive content; about 40 % know sb who has experienced cyberbullying* – ______		
main part		
	pros	**cons**
argument 1	______	______
reasons and examples that **support argument 1**	a) *force websites to block bullies and to delete offensive content* b) ______	a) *can be shared very quickly + reaches large audience* b) ______
argument 2	______	______
reasons and examples that **support argument 2**	*workshops about 'online rules': communication rules apply online too; careful with private information*	*cyberbullies often haven't learned how to deal with their emotions, need sth they don't get (love, attention, help ...), or don't know how powerful words can be – no law or educational workshop can simply fix this*
conclusion		
______		

1 punishment ['pʌnɪʃmənt] the act of making sb suffer because they have broken the law or done something wrong

b) *Read these example introductions for the essay on cyberbullying. Which is better? Explain why.*

A Have you ever received offensive messages? Has anyone ever posted embarrassing photos of you? These are examples of cyberbullying, a form of attack that should be stopped since using social media is an important part of everyday life. Some people say it can be done. But is that really true?

B Today most people use social media and cyberbullying is a terrible problem which affects lots of people, especially teenagers like me. I hate cyberbullying because it's an awful thing which should be stopped as soon as possible.

c) *Read these example first paragraphs. Which is better? Explain why.*

A My argument is that we could change the laws to fight cyberbullying. Websites and apps could be forced to block bullies and delete offensive comments and pictures. Why aren't we doing this already? If there were just really harsh punishments for bullies, this would be a thing of the past.

B Changing laws could be one way to approach the problem of cyberbullying. For example, websites and apps could be forced to block bullies and to delete offensive content. There could also be harsher punishments for bullies. These are just some of the possibilities for putting a stop to or at least reducing cyberbullying.

d) *Finish the essay. Write the paragraph for pro-argument 2, the paragraphs for the con-arguments, and the conclusion.*

e) *Exchange texts with a partner. Peer-edit each other's work with the help of this checklist.*

Checklist: Essay

Structure:
- introduction, main part, conclusion
- main part divided into paragraphs
- paragraphs start with a topic sentence

Language:
- easy to read and understand
- correct spelling and grammar
- use of linking words

Content:
- strong, convincing arguments
- support for each pro / con (examples, reasons, statistics …)

Writing skills

The conclusion repeats the main question using other words or sums up your opinion. You may also suggest solutions, warn of possible consequences or encourage readers to reach their own conclusion.
Do not introduce new arguments.

Tip

Give constructive feedback:
- Start with what you liked about your partner's essay.
- Always try to give tips on how to correct mistakes and improve the structure, language and content.

On these pages you are going to practise doing the types of tasks you will do in the ZP10 (*Zentrale Prüfung Klasse 10, Nordrhein-Westfalen*). You are also going to get some useful tips on how to deal with the tasks successfully.

A15 1 Listening: Virtual fashion

Read the statements. Then listen to part of a radio programme about 'virtual fashion'. While you are listening, tick ✔ the correct box. Then listen again and check your answers.

1. Nike is going to …
   a) ☐ start producing virtual sneakers.
   b) ☐ increase production of virtual sneakers.
   c) ☐ buy a producer of virtual sneakers.

2. The Business of Fashion …
   a) ☐ publishes information about the fashion industry.
   b) ☐ regulates the fashion industry.
   c) ☐ advises fashion companies.

3. According to Imran Amed, …
   a) ☐ virtual fashion has always been important.
   b) ☐ virtual fashions are often exaggerated.
   c) ☐ any kind of appearance is possible with virtual fashion.

4. The presenter gives examples of clothes that are …
   a) ☐ as exciting as real-world fashions.
   b) ☐ not physically possible.
   c) ☐ already being sold in virtual form.

5. Amed thinks virtual fashion offers …
   a) ☐ endless possibilities for making a statement about oneself.
   b) ☐ a way to make a lot of money.
   c) ☐ hope for the fashion industry.

6. Amed says the purpose of fashion is to …
   a) ☐ make those who wear it feel good about themselves.
   b) ☐ make a lifestyle statement.
   c) ☐ show the personality of those who wear it.

7. People want to use virtual fashion in …
   a) ☐ a similar way to physical fashion.
   b) ☐ a totally different way to physical fashion.
   c) ☐ a huge variety of different ways.

8. Fashion company bosses understand that younger buyers will …
   a) ☐ spend more time in virtual environments in the future.
   b) ☐ be important for future sales.
   c) ☐ create the future's virtual worlds.

9. Younger fashion buyers …
   a) ☐ are more comfortable in virtual environments.
   b) ☐ see less difference between physical and virtual environments.
   c) ☐ love virtual fashion.

Tip

In the audio, you won't find any of the key words in the questions. This means that it's not a clever strategy to just listen for certain words and try to guess the answers that way. Instead, try to stay calm (e.g. by taking three deep breaths in and out before listening) and understand the gist of what is said. This should make it easier to find the correct answers.

2 Vocabulary: The Raspberry Pi

The Raspberry Pi is a very cheap, small computer which is mainly used for educational purposes. Fill in suitable words or tick ✔ the correct box. Give only one solution.

1. Raspberry Pi is a series of very cheap miniature computers ______________________ in the UK by a charity called 'Raspberry Pi Foundation'.
   a) ☐ perpetuated b) ☐ determined c) ☐ enabled d) ☐ developed
2. The price starts at around just £15 for the most basic model, and goes up from there depending on the ______________________ specifications.
   a) ☐ technical b) ☐ mechanical c) ☐ practical d) ☐ electronic
3. Users can connect a screen, ______________________, mouse, camera etc.
4. They can get free ______________________ to make the device work as a computer.
5. The project aims to ______________________ teaching and learning computer science.
   a) ☐ ensure b) ☐ promote c) ☐ deliver d) ☐ process
6. Younger students may previously have done everything in their digital lives by ______________________ a touchscreen.
   a) ☐ hitting b) ☐ pressing c) ☐ typing d) ☐ tapping
7. The Raspberry Pi offers an affordable way for students to learn ______________________ skills.
   a) ☐ coding b) ☐ coder c) ☐ coded d) ☐ code
8. They can create new apps and ______________________ them on specific online platforms for other users to try.
9. They can also write new programmes or ______________________ existing programmes to control machines and electronic devices that they have built themselves.
   a) ☐ regulate b) ☐ adopt c) ☐ adapt d) ☐ retouch
10. In ______________________, many apps that work on a 'normal' computer will work on a Raspberry Pi. These include web browsers, image editors and word processing programmes.
11. It is possible to use a Raspberry Pi for a huge variety of digital activities, from sending an email or writing a presentation to creating computer-______________________ images and making music.
12. An exception is gaming. Although they can be connected to a gaming ______________________, these tiny computers are not powerful enough for playing most of the latest video games.

Tip

The topic and words in this Vocabulary part are usually relevant for the Writing task that follows. Remember this when you are working on the Writing tasks: you can always come back here and get inspired by this topic vocabulary.

3 Writing: Click'd

Teenagers Allie and Nathan both love to code and have great coding skills. After many months of hard work, Nathan has just published a new game called Built *and it's very successful.*

"These aren't test characters." He tapped his finger on the glass. "Real, actual people are making them move and build and buy things." He turned to her. "There are real people playing my game. Can you believe that? And look at this." Nathan switched screens and his browser filled with news stories he'd collected from a Google search. She read the headlines.

Playing for Good

Teens Change the Game

What a Difference a Game Makes

"These articles have been coming in all day, and every single one includes screenshots and the download link for Built."

"Hey," Allie said. "I know you're thrilled[1] that real people are playing Built, but do you know where else there are real people?" She tipped her head toward the door. "Outside. In the quad. There's also this thing called sun."

She formed a circle with her hands. "Big yellow thing. Hangs out in the sky during the day. Perhaps you've heard of it?"

"Eh ... sun, shmun. I like it in here. It's quiet. And we have snacks." He reached for his bag of microwave popcorn and stuffed a handful into his mouth.

Allie took the bag away and set it on her side of the table, out of his reach.

"You need to get out of here, Nathan. Go to the quad. Find your friends."

He shook his head. "No thanks."

Allie leaned in closer. "Why not?"

He shrugged[2]. "I don't even know where I'd go."

Allie felt like her heart might break into a million little pieces.

"I saw Cory and Mark on my way here. They're sitting at a table next to the basketball courts."

He forced a laugh. "And what am I supposed to do, sit down and join them?

"Yeah. Why not?"

"Because I've barely talked to them in over a year. We say hi in the halls and stuff, but it's not like I can sit down and start chatting like we're all old friends."

"But you are old friends. You've known them all your life. You'll see. Once you sit down it will be easy. Just show them your game, tell them about the competition, and talk about all your new users and the news coverage you're getting today. You're famous! You're *Naaaate*." She drew out the name and he turned toward her and smiled.

"You make it sound easy," he said.

"It will be. I promise." Allie rested her elbows on her knees and leaned in closer to him. "Come on. I'll help you."

Nathan sighed[3]. "Fine."

He followed Allie out of the lab and into the hallway. They walked in silence until they reached the quad.

"See, they're right down there," she said, but when she looked over at Nathan, all the color seemed to have drained[4] from his face.

"Lunch is almost over now. I'll go up to them tomorrow." He started to walk away, but Allie grabbed his arm. She wasn't about to let him off the hook[5] that easily. "Nate." He locked his eyes on her. "You can do this."

"I'm ridiculously nervous." He held his hand out in front of him, and she could see it trembling[6].

1 thrilled [θrɪld] very happy ○ **2** to shrug [ʃrʌg] to raise and lower your shoulders to say you don't know sth ○ **3** to sigh [saɪ] to breathe out slowly, making a noise ○ **4** to drain [dreɪn] to remove elements like water or blood ○ **5** to let sb off the hook [ˌlɜt ɔf ðə 'huk] to let sb get out of a difficult situation ○ **6** to tremble ['trembl] to shake, e.g. because you're afraid

Allie rested her hand on the back of his. She wrapped her fingers around it.

"On the count of three," she said.

He drew in a breath. "One."

"Two."

"Three," he said, and she dropped his hand.

"Go."

She watched him walk across the quad. He ran his hand through his hair a few times and adjusted his T-shirt. At one point, he stopped, and she wondered if he was going to turn around and chicken out. But he kept walking.

When he got close enough, he stopped. He said something, and Cory and Mark turned around. They smiled. And then they scooted over to make room between them.

From: Tamara Ireland Stone, *Click'd*, 2019 (abridged and adapted)

Read the tasks carefully. Make sure to write about all the aspects presented in each task.

a) ***Describe*** *the situation Nathan is in and how he deals with it.*

b) **Analyse** *how information about Nathan's character is conveyed to the reader. In doing so, look at the way the story is told (narrative perspective).*

c) *Here you can choose between three different options. Do only* ***one*** *of them.*

Option 1:

"Young people under the age of 18 should limit their screen time to three hours a day."

Comment on the statement from **your** point of view and include the following aspects:
- reasons in favour of and against this statement,
- examples to support your arguments,
- the amount of time you spend looking at screens, and your feelings about this.

Or

Option 2:

Allie, Cory and Mark have a fun time with Nathan. **Write a continuation** of the story.
Include the following aspects:
- what the four of them do together,
- how Nathan reacts,
- what Nathan learns from the experience.

Start: 'Hey," said Cory. "I've just had a great idea. Why don't the four of us …?"

Or

Option 3:

Write a diary entry for Nathan.
Include the following aspects:
- the events in the extract from his point of view,
- his feelings about them,
- what he learns from the experience.

Start:
Dear Diary,
I realised something important today.
For the last few months, I've been …

Tip

Choosing an option
Can't decide which option to choose in the last part? Do a quick brainstorming activity and find out where you have more or better ideas. Usually, there is one task where you have to write an objective, factual text, and one that is more creative. Think about which type of task is usually easier for you.

1 Cultural diversity → SB 83/3

READING

a) *Read the Across cultures box that introduces different metaphors for cultural diversity.*

Across cultures

Canada is often described with the 'mosaic' metaphor. It expresses the idea that many cultural groups live there side by side, welcoming diversity while preserving at least some parts of the different traditional cultures. Some people compare countries like this to a salad bowl. The US is another example of a big country with many different nations and cultures. The US society is often called a 'melting pot', where cultural identities combine to form something new.

WRITING

b) *Think about the society you live in. Say which metaphor describes it best, or create your own. Think about: How is cultural diversity seen and lived in your country? In your everyday life, how do you experience that you live in a culturally diverse society? Make notes in your exercise book.*

c) *Visualize your ideas in b). Draw a mosaic, salad bowl, melting pot, or your own metaphor, and label it with the things that make the society you live in 'multicultural'.*

VOCABULARY

2 Canada vocabulary → SB 84/5

Complete the puzzle.

A

B

C

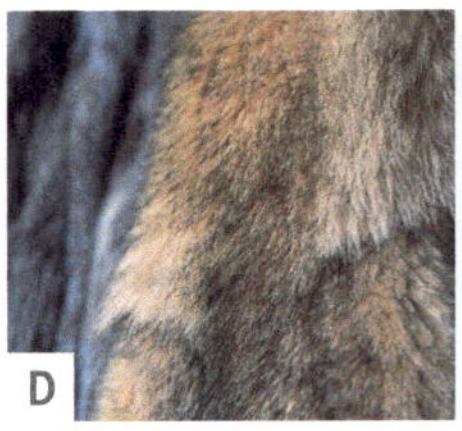
D

E

Down ↓

1 describes people whose ancestors lived in a place before it was colonised
2 photo A
4 photo B
5 photo C
6 type of school for the children of First Nations peoples in Canada
7 photo D

Across →

3 was paid to victims of the residential schools system
6 area where First Nations peoples in Canada were forced to live
8 photo E
9 important industry in Canada (clue: trees)
10 far from places where many people live; describes much of Canada
11 Canada has six of them. If it's 6 p.m. in Germany, it can be a time between 9 a.m. and 1:30 p.m. in Canada.

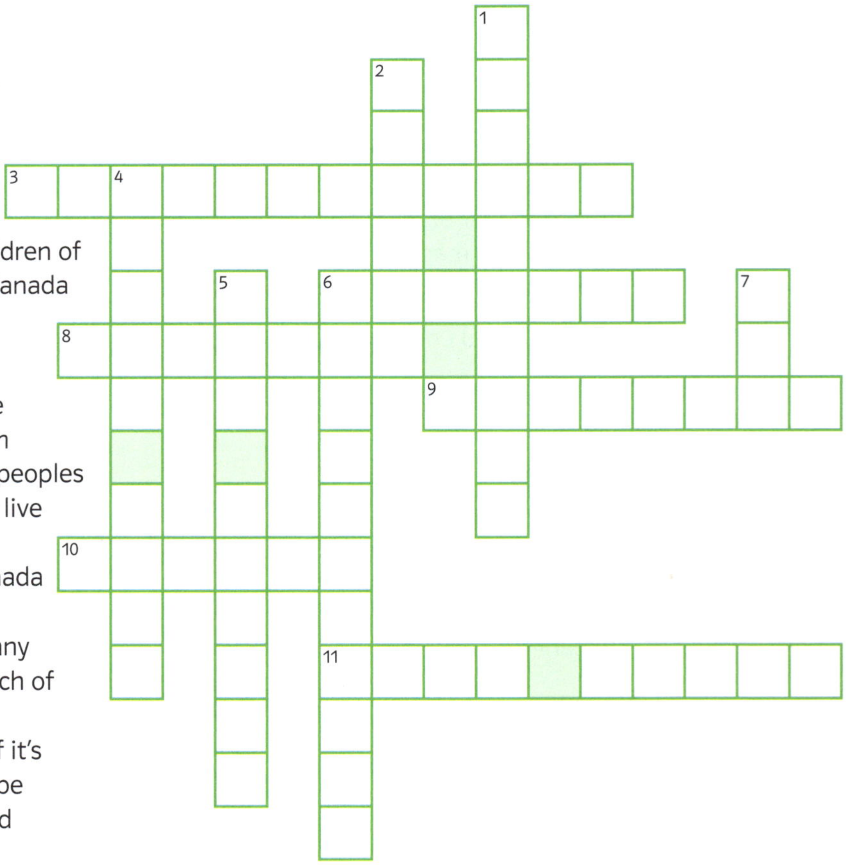

Unit 3 Discover Canada!

VOCABULARY

1 Word families → SB 86/2; S2

a) *Write down the correct word from the same word family. You can use a dictionary for help.*

to adapt (verb) → ______________________ (noun)

Asia (noun) → ______________________ (adjective)

constitutional (adjective) → ______________________ (noun)

faith (noun) → ______________________ (adjective)

to extract (verb) → ______________________ (noun)

to deposit (verb) → ______________________ (noun)

b) *In your exercise book, write your own example sentence with each of the words that you added.*

LISTENING

2 Maple syrup from Sugar Field Farm → SB 87/3; S29

A16

a) *Listen to the tour of Sugar Field Farm. What information does the tour guide Andrew give about sap[1] and maple syrup? Underline the correct answers.* ***More than one*** *answer may be correct.*

1. **Sap** is the same colour as maple syrup. | is like blood in a human. | has 2–5 % sugar. | should be collected during the Sugar Moon.
2. **Maple syrup** was always the main business of Sugar Field Farm. | was first made by European settlers. | is produced by separating sugar and water. | is made in a completely different way today.

b) *Listen again. Complete this part of a flyer about Sugar Field Farm.*

The best time to collect sap is between __________________ and __________________.

You can start when the nights are __________________ degrees and the days are around __________________ degrees Celsius. You have to __________________ collecting sap when the trees get __________________. The next steps are: making the sap come out by putting a piece of plastic or metal in the tree (the Indigenous people used __________________), collecting the sap in __________________ and leaving the sap outside at night so that the water turns into __________________. Our guests can try out a __________________ that especially __________________ love: You pour maple syrup on __________________ and roll a __________________ in it. Delicious!

1 sap [sæp] sth that flows inside a tree

VOCABULARY

3 Words from Leon's blog → SB 89/1

Match the verbs on the left with the words on the right.

1. to do	a) bikes
2. to be	b) the host
3. to rent	c) some kayaking
4. to board	d) the view
5. to enjoy	e) power
6. to provide	f) by accident
7. to stay	g) a ferry
8. to find sth	h) overnight

GRAMMAR

4 ‹More about Montreal› → SB 89/3; ‹G13, G14›

At the end of his trip around Canada with his parents, Leon is writing an email to his host family about the end of their last day in Montreal. Complete his email with ***tenses referring to the past****.*

Dear Julie, John, Phillip and Peyton,

we ______________________ (to travel) around Canada for seven days already. It sure doesn't feel like it, time flies by! Let me tell you about our second and last day in Montreal a couple of days ago. It ______________________ (to be) exhausting. We all felt tired because we ______________________ (to do) lots of sightseeing all day. My feet hurt as I ______________________ (to walk) a lot more than usual. We ______________________ (to speak) French since we ______________________ (to arrive), so we ______________________ (to look forward to) getting a break from that soon. Dad loved the ice hockey match even though he really ______________________ (not to expect) to go to one. I'm surprised that we ______________________ (to see) everything we ______________________ (to plan) to see – our programme was tough! We decided to go to bed early because we ______________________ (to get up) early every day of the trip. We ______________________ (to love) every minute in Montreal even though we hadn't been expecting it to be as interesting as Toronto.

See you soon!

Leon

Tip

You already know these tenses referring to the past:
- present perfect simple (*has / have done*)
- present perfect progressive (*has / have been doing*
- simple past (*did*)
- past progressive (*was / were doing*)
- past perfect simple (*had done*)
- past perfect progressive (*had been doing*)

GRAMMAR

5 ‹Leon's plans› → SB 90/4; ‹G13, G14, G15›

a) *Before Leon left to travel around Canada with his parents, he told his host sister Peyton about his plans. What does Peyton tell her parents the next day? Use **indirect speech** with **backshift**.*

1. "We've been looking forward to our trip for ages."

   Leon said that ______________________________

2. "We're not going to try and see everything in Canada."

   He told me ______________________________

3. "I've done lots of research about the places we're planning to visit."

   He mentioned that ______________________________

4. "I'll call you when we know exactly how long we expect to be away."

   He said ______________________________

b) *Remember the last time you were in a foreign city, country or any other new place. Talk to a partner about:*

where you went | what you experienced (things you saw and heard, feelings, smells) | a funny / interesting / embarrassing situation

c) *Tell your partner's story to another partner. Use indirect speech with backshift.*

6 Video CVs → SB 90/6; S16, S21

VOCABULARY

a) *Leon's friend Bohdan is applying for an exchange programme to work in Canada during the summer. Complete his personal profile.*

enjoy | free time | good | hard | organised | placement | skills | strength | teamwork | volunteer

I did a six-week work experience ______________ in a local design studio. I have done ______________ work for a local environmental charity. I have ______________ communication and IT ______________. I am ______________-working and well-______________. I believe my main ______________ is that I have great ______________ skills. In my ______________, I ______________ sports activities including kayaking and ice hockey.

SPEAKING

MK

b) *Bohdan is expected to send a video CV to the exchange organisation. Discuss these questions about video CVs.*

1. In what situations might you want to make a video CV?
2. What are the advantages and disadvantages of a video CV?
3. What do you think are the characteristics of good and bad video CVs?

c) *You are applying for a place on a student exchange to Canada. Make a video CV for yourself. Then show it to a partner and give each other feedback.*

MEDIATION

7 Tips for an exchange interview → SB 90/7; S34

Your friend has been invited to an interview for a student exchange programme with Canada and is worried about preparing properly for the interview. She wonders what questions the interviewers will ask and how to make the interviewers like her. You find this article online. Write a message to her in German in which you try to help her with these points.

9 tips for a student exchange interview

1. Get into the right mental state
To stay calm in the weeks and days before the interview, take the pressure off yourself by putting it into perspective. Even if the interview is a disaster, you can apply for a different programme, apply for the same programme next year or do something completely different. Remember the old saying: 'When one door closes, another opens'. It is also important not to overestimate the competition. Why wouldn't you be as good as most of the other candidates?

2. Review your application before the interview
It is likely that the interviewers will want to discuss what you have written about yourself. Make sure you remember what you wrote, and prepare more to say about those things. For example, if you said that you have good communication skills, think of examples. If you have mentioned volunteer work, what exactly was that work? In what ways was doing it good for you?

3. Learn about the organisation and the programme
Find out about the objectives and structure of the organisation. Why do they organise exchanges? What benefits do they see in exchanges? How well do your objectives fit with theirs?

4. Research the destination
Learn about the culture of and general facts about the country you hope to visit. You are likely to be asked why you would like to spend time there. Be able to give an answer which shows you have done research.

5. Prepare answers to typical questions
Think about how you would answer the most common interview questions. These include:
- Tell us about yourself.
- Why do you want to go on an exchange?
- Why would you be a good exchange student?
- Why are you interested in an exchange in that specific country or region?
- How would you deal with any problems with the host family?

6. Find out about the location and arrive on time
Avoid stress on the day of the interview by planning every detail of your journey to the location. Allow enough time. If the interview is in a large building, try to find a map of it online to help you get to the right room.

7. Make a good first impression
People often form opinions of others within the first few seconds of meeting. Do your best to start the interview well. Greet and address people appropriately. This may mean shaking each person's hand and addressing them as 'Ms X' and 'Mr Y' once they have introduced themselves.

8. Behave with the interviewers in a professional way
Don't try to 'make friends with' the interviewers with very informal language or jokes. Follow them and be as formal or informal as they are. They may be very serious and formal, relaxed and friendly or somewhere in between. Keep eye contact with the person who is talking to you. Answer questions fully and carefully, but avoid very long answers. Don't argue. If you are corrected, you can say something like, 'Thank you, I didn't know that.'

9. Make a good final impression
At the end of the interview, you may be asked if you have any questions. If you have a relevant question, it can be a good opportunity to make more of an impression. Never ask whether the interview was successful, or when you will hear their decision – this could seem rude. As you leave, thank the interviewers for inviting you.

LISTENING

8 Energy and the environment → SB 92/1; S29

A17

a) *Listen to the report about energy and the environment in British Columbia. Ben Lavoie interviews Liz Wilson, a member of the Fort Nelson First Nation, and Amanda Jacobs, an energy expert. Tick ✔ the correct answer.*

1. Which problem does Ben not mention?
   a) ☐ Animals can't find enough food.
   b) ☐ It's hotter than it used to be.
   c) ☐ Trees are dying from diseases.

2. Fracking …
   a) ☐ helps to reach more gas and oil.
   b) ☐ kills all animals around.
   c) ☐ needs wind and water.

3. Fracking uses a mix of …
   a) ☐ rock, oil and gas.
   b) ☐ chemicals, sand and water.
   c) ☐ rock, chemicals and water.

4. Through fracking, Fort Nelson First Nation …
   a) ☐ has improved a lot.
   b) ☐ will always have enough jobs.
   c) ☐ has lost more than they have won.

b) *Read the questions. Then listen again and give short answers.*

1. What positive aspect of fracking does Liz mention?

____

2. What has happened to the lake in Fort Nelson?

____

3. What has caused these problems?

____

4. How did the wildlife react to the fracking? Why?

____

5. What do these numbers refer to?

87 %	
21 million	
85 million	
60 %	
2	
$22 billion	

c) *Name three of Amanda's ideas on how everybody can help the environment.*

____

____

d) *Use the information from a)–c) and your own ideas to write and role-play a conversation between Liz Wilson from Fort Nelson and the manager of the fracking company.*

VOCABULARY

9 Eco-tourism in Canada → SB 92/2

Complete the post on a tourism blog. Change the form of the word where necessary.

chemicals | to contribute | to encourage | to endanger | to extract | fossil fuel | habitat | to put sth into practice | to retreat | stream

Millions of tourists visit Canada every year. This ____________ millions of dollars to the economy, but it is not such good news for the environment. Transporting the tourists uses large amounts of ____________, and visitors can ____________ the ____________ of the amazing wildlife they have come to see. Canada has other environmental problems too, of course. The glaciers are ____________, rivers and ____________ are polluted with ____________, and beautiful landscapes are destroyed to ____________ oil, resulting in major disturbances to the environment. The government actively ____________ eco-tourism, and many sustainable tourism ideas have been ____________. However, the list of problems is long and there is definitely a long way to go.

GRAMMAR

10 ‹Tar sands[1]› → SB 92/3; ‹G16›

Complete the article about tar sands with the ***expressions of probability****. More than one expression may be possible. Choose the* ***one*** *you think is best for each gap, and use each expression once.*

to be certain to | to be likely to | to be said to | to be supposed to | to happen to

Tar sands production uses large amounts of land, water and energy to extract oil from sandy ground. It ____________ be one of the worst forms of energy production for the environment. Canada ____________ have the world's largest tar sands deposits. Tar sands extraction is a big business in Canada, and ____________ remain so for many years to come. Like most countries, Canada ____________ be reducing its CO_2 emissions, and tar sands extraction does not fit in with this objective. There is strong local opposition to tar sands projects, and this ____________ almost ____________ continue.

1 tar sands ['tɑː sændz] a mixture of sand, minerals, water and oil

GRAMMAR **11**

⟨All about you …⟩

→ SB 92/4; ⟨G16⟩

Write sentences about yourself with ***expressions of probability****.*

1. Something that you are (not) likely to do in the future.

   I am ______________________________

2. Something that you are (almost) certain to do in the future.

   I am ______________________________

3. Something which you are supposed to do, but don't always do.

   I am ______________________________

4. Something which is often / sometimes said to be true about your neighbourhood / town / city / area / state / country / culture by some people, but which you disagree with.

   ____

5. Something which happened to you by chance. Start with the time: *A few days ago, … Last year, …* etc.

   ____

SPEAKING **12**

Photo competition

→ SB 93/5; S11

a) *Look at the photos. They take part in a Canadian photo competition and should raise awareness of environmental issues in Canada. Discuss the statement that each photo makes. Decide which photo you like best and explain your choice.*

A

B

C

D

E

F

b) *Find one or more other photos to enter the competition. Give each other feedback.*

WRITING
13 A cartoon
→ SB 93/6; S13

a) *Describe and analyse the cartoon. Use your exercise book.*

Useful phrases

the Arctic | ice | cactus | desert | climate change | I knew that things were … | I didn't expect to see … | This must be a sign of … | We're going to have to …

"Whoa. Now **this** is a bad sign."

b) *Write a short dialogue for the two polar bears. Use your exercise book.*

VOCABULARY
14 Talking about countries and regions
→ SB 93/7

Sort the words into the correct categories. Some words may fit more than one category.

mountains | glacier | lake | warm | forest | temperature | tropical | immigration | to increase | mild | desert | age | sea | gender | heatwave | cold | to grow | density | hot | average | fields | drought | hills | temperate | to decrease | nationality | growth | precipitation | Arctic | conditions | dry | beach | cool

landscape	climate	population

SPEAKING
15 Your turn: Make your own video
→ SB 94/4; S16

MK

Do some research on a tradition in your region. Make a short video for your partner school in the UK and explain its history and background.

Tip

Use interviews, visual materials and real objects to make your video more interesting.

The Outside Circle → SB 119/8; S1, S2

In the extract from the graphic novel The Outside Circle *by Patti LaBoucane-Benson, a group of First Nations men with criminal records are taking part in a programme led by two elders, Elder Violet and Elder Roy. The programme is designed to help the men deal with their strong feelings like anger and sadness – symptoms of these generational trauma from which they suffer since their traditions were stolen from them. Pete is one of these men. He killed his mother's boyfriend in a fight, just after he had decided to leave his pregnant girlfriend – a story that has repeated itself in his family (Pete's father also left).*

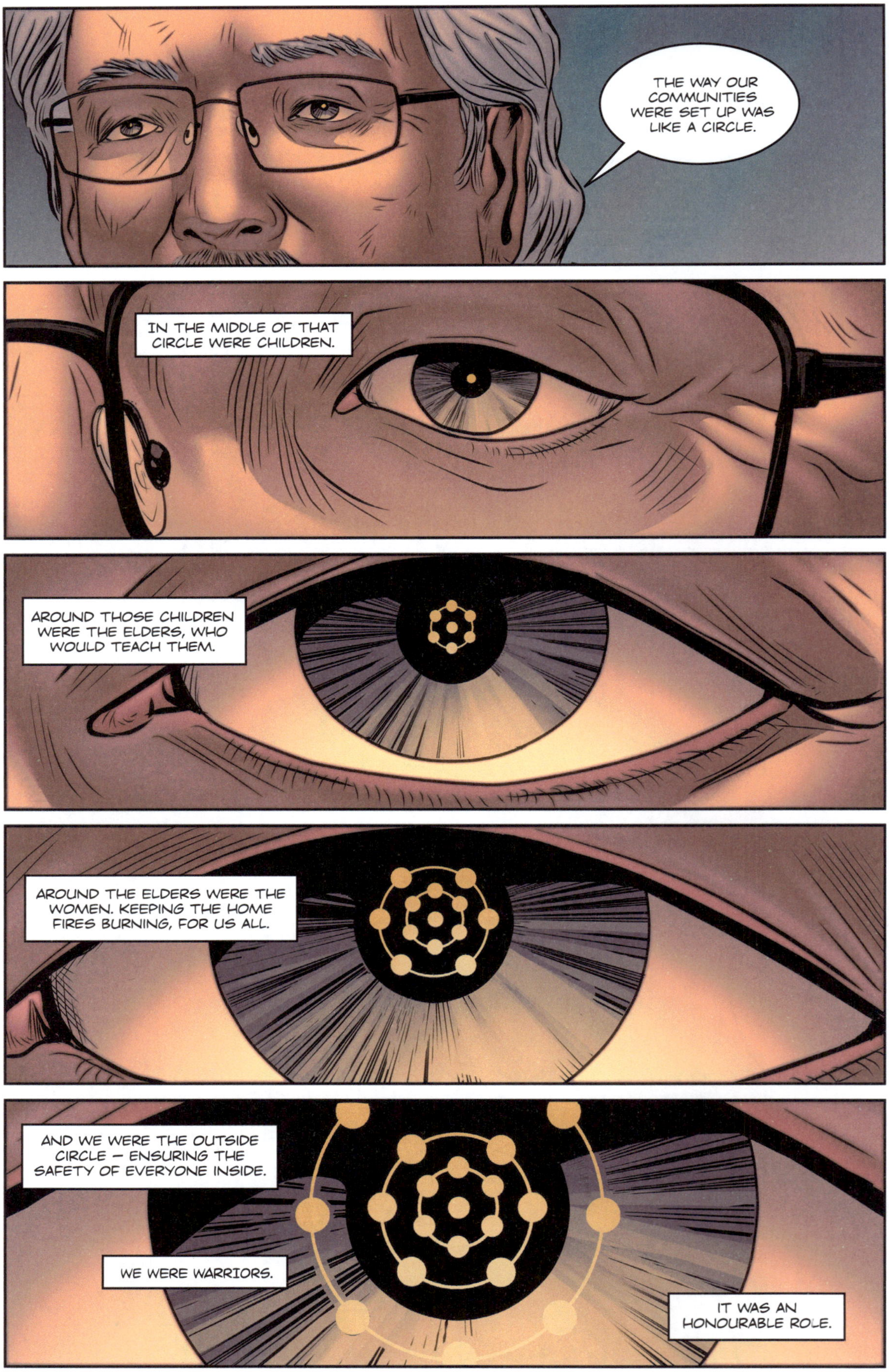
THE WAY OUR COMMUNITIES WERE SET UP WAS LIKE A CIRCLE.
IN THE MIDDLE OF THAT CIRCLE WERE CHILDREN.
AROUND THOSE CHILDREN WERE THE ELDERS, WHO WOULD TEACH THEM.
AROUND THE ELDERS WERE THE WOMEN. KEEPING THE HOME FIRES BURNING, FOR US ALL.
AND WE WERE THE OUTSIDE CIRCLE – ENSURING THE SAFETY OF EVERYONE INSIDE.
WE WERE WARRIORS.
IT WAS AN HONOURABLE ROLE.

SO WHAT HAPPENED TO OUR SACRED ROLE? MANY OF YOU AROUND THIS FIRE ONLY KNOW WHAT IT MEANS TO BE A PREDATOR AND BULLY.
IT'S ALL ABOUT POWER AND CONTROL. WE PREY ON THE WEAK – WOMEN, CHILDREN, AND THE ELDERLY – TO GET WHAT WE WANT.
SO MANY OF US GREW UP WITHOUT DADS AND HAVE NEVER BEEN TAUGHT ABOUT OUR RESPONSIBILITY AS MEN.
I'M NOT HERE TO BLAME YOU. I WAS THE SAME WAY.
BUT US MEN DON'T KNOW ***WHAT WE DON'T KNOW*** AND OUR COMMUNITIES ARE SUFFERING.
THESE DAYS, WHO'S PROTECTING OUR WOMEN AND CHILDREN?
IT'S SAD TO SAY, BUT USUALLY THEY NEED PROTECTION FROM US.
HOW MANY SINGLE MOMS ARE OUT THERE ON THEIR OWN AND ON WELFARE BECAUSE NO DAD HAS STEPPED UP TO THE PLATE?
AND WHAT ARE CHILDREN LEARNING FROM THEIR DADS THAT AREN'T AROUND? WHAT DID YOU LEARN FROM YOUR FATHERS?
IN ORDER TO UNDERSTAND YOUR ROLE AS MEN, YOU HAVE TO LEARN ABOUT THE SACRED ROLE OF WOMEN IN OUR SOCIETY.
WOMEN ARE THE GIVERS OF LIFE. THEY NURTURE US AS CHILDREN AND TEACH US RIGHT FROM WRONG.
AND LET'S FACE IT: WITHOUT WOMEN, WE MEN ARE LOST.
WE CANNOT BE PROTECTORS AND PROVIDERS WITHOUT STRONG WOMEN BESIDE US.
MEN AND WOMEN HAVE TO SUPPORT EACH OTHER TO HAVE A GOOD LIFE – AN HONOURABLE LIFE.
AND NOW WE WILL GO INTO THE SWEAT AND PRAY FOR THE CREATOR TO HELP US TO BE GOOD MEN . . .

READING

16 Your reaction → SB 119/8; S1, S2

MK

a) *Read the extract from the graphic novel. In your exercise book, write down your first reactions. Give your ideas about what the topics and themes of the whole graphic novel may be.*

b) *Research the author, Patti LaBoucane-Benson. Find out about her career, especially her research about historic trauma healing programmes, and her graphic novel* The Outside Circle *(the story, her inspiration and motivation). Then explain if your findings change your reaction to the extract and if so, how.*

READING

17 Understanding the story → SB 119/8; S1, S2

a) *Put the points in the order that Elder Roy makes them. Number them 1–9.*

- ☐ Men need to understand the importance of women's role in society.
- ☐ When the boys became older adults, they helped to teach the next generation of boys.
- ☐ Some First Nations men struggle with fatherhood.
- ☐ Everybody in the community had a role and worked together.
- ☐ In the past, First Nations boys went through a ceremony to become adult men.
- ☐ Many First Nations men grew up without fathers to act as role models.
- ☐ Men need strong women to support them.
- ☐ Some First Nations men have forgotten their traditional roles in their communities.
- ☐ The ceremony showed that the men could be useful members of their communities.

b) *Draw a diagram that represents First Nations communities as described by Elder Roy.*

c) *Sum up the concepts of family, gender and community that Elder Roy describes.*

WRITING

18 Analysis: Atmosphere and themes → SB 119/8; S4, S11

Answer these questions in your exercise book.

1. Analyse the atmosphere that is created in the extract. Include an analysis of the effect of the colouring and the design of the panels in your answer.
2. Analyse the way that images of other scenes are combined with the main scene around the fire. Explain what these other scenes symbolise and the effect they have.
3. Analyse the use of shapes and forms. Include the circle around the fire and what Elder Roy says about the structure of a traditional community. How do the shapes communicate concepts?
4. Analyse the way the text introduces issues and avoids judging First Nations men for their actions.

19 Options → SB 119/8; S17, S32

*Choose **one** of the following tasks.*

WRITING

a) *Pete sends his brother a text message after the scene in the extract. What does he write? How does he feel, especially about the traditional social structures that Elder Roy presented?*

SPEAKING

b) *Research Canada's colonial past. Then discuss how the problems and issues described in the extract are connected with Canada's colonial history. Share examples of similar problems in other post-colonial[2] societies.*

1 to heal [hiːl] to become / make sth healthy again ○ 2 post-colonial [ˌpəʊst kəˈləʊniəl] referring to the time after the end of colonial rule

20 Setting the scene → SB 120/1

Read these two beginnings for an audio adaptation of the extract from The Outside Circle. *Decide which one is better and say why.*

Media skills

FX is an abbreviation used in media and film and usually means 'effects'.

1. **FX: A CAMPFIRE BURNING**

Narrator: It is a cold, dark night. A group of nine men and one older woman are standing in a circle around a campfire. The woman introduces one of the men.

Woman: This is Elder Roy. I brought him here to speak to you about some men's business.

2. **FX: A CAMPFIRE BURNING (CONTINUES UNDER DIALOGUE)**

Narrator: Nine men and an older woman are standing close together in a circle around a big campfire, trying to keep warm in the cold night air. It is dark all around, but the light of the fire shows the serious expressions on their faces. The rest of the group is waiting for the woman to introduce a grey-haired man that they haven't seen before.

Woman: This is Elder Roy. I brought him here to speak to you about some men's business.

21 Adding extra information → SB 120/2

a) *For an audio adaptation, you may need to add extra information to include more details from the original text based on the visuals. Find places in the extract to add this information, and continue the sentences in your exercise book.*

1. The other men in the circle listen silently and imagine scenes of …
2. A young man with a scar on his face looks down at the ground and remembers his …

b) *You can also add extra information from the narrator to remind the listener of the scene and to break up long dialogue parts. Find places in the extract to add extra information and continue the sentences.*

1. Elder Roy stops talking. The other men …
2. One of the younger men puts another piece of wood on the fire and …

c) *Find places where it may also be useful to add extra lines of dialogue. Explain who could say them and how they may be useful.*

1. Thanks to all of you for being here this evening.
2. Let's stand a little closer to the fire. It really is cold tonight.

22 Defining the characters → SB 120/4

Complete the grid with your ideas.

character	sex and age of the character	language / accent
Elder Violet ('WOMAN')		
Elder Roy		
Pete ('young man with a scar')*		
Pete's mom (in the photo)*		
Pete's pregnant girlfriend (second last panel)		

*If added as speaking parts

23 Prepare and write your script → SB 121/Steps 1–2; S36

Work in small groups. Write a script for an audio adaptation of the extract. You can use your ideas from p. 59 and / or use your own ideas.

24 Prepare the sound effects → SB 121/Steps 3–4; S35

MK

Find suitable sound effects in Creative Commons licence sources:

- a large campfire burning
- a remote place at night (e.g. light wind, a dog barks in the distance)
- any other sound effects you want to use

25 Practise the speaking parts → SB 121/Step 5

Practise the speaking parts. While you are practising, make a note of any aspects of your script that could be better. Then improve your script.

26 Record and edit your audio adaptation → SB 121/Steps 6–8

MK

Record the audio adaptation. If you need a tool for editing, search for 'free audio editor'. These tools are available for smartphones, tablets and computers. They allow you to record the speaking parts and sound effects on different tracks, to edit them afterwards and to record parts again if necessary. Record yourself saying a few phrases to learn how to use the tool. Then add a sound effect on another track.

Media skills

When you record:
- record in a quiet place without background noise
- do a sound check to make sure the speakers are close enough to the microphone(s)
- act natural

When you edit:
- make sure the sound effects aren't too loud / the dialogue isn't too quiet
- slow down dialogue by adding short gaps between parts of it
- check that it's clear what the sound effects represent

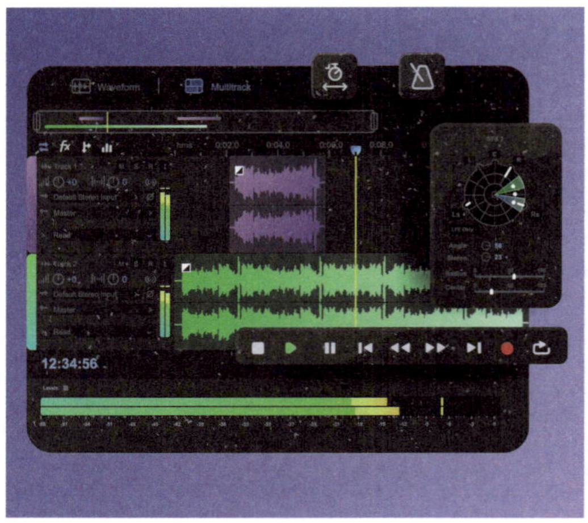

27 Give and ask for feedback → SB 121/Step 9

Play your recording to another group. Give each other feedback:

- What did you like about the audio adaptation?
- What was hard to understand?
- What could they have done differently or better?

Can you . . . ?

Stelle mithilfe des Bewertungsbogens im Beihefter auf Seite 29 fest, was du schon kannst oder noch üben musst.

Dealing with plays

LISTENING

1 Putting on a school play → SB 130/1; S29

A18

Listen to a school podcast about staging a school play. Write answers to the questions.

1. Why does Abigail have some experience of professional theatre productions?

2. What is the main difference between staging a professional production and a school play?

3. What is Abigail doing for the school play?

4. How was the playscript produced?

5. Who is directing the play?

6. Why would the school's style of production be a risk in a professional theatre?

7. What genre is the production, and why?

8. What does Abigail's mother think of the production process?

WRITING

2 Talking about a theatre production → SB 130/2; S35

MK

a) *Your exchange school's drama club has asked for suggestions about what to perform next. Research a play or musical you have seen or would like to see. Find out about the following elements:*

- plot, setting, characters
- themes
- playwright
- music and lyrics (if any)
- director and cast of first / a famous production
- set and costumes
- reviews

b) *Write a reply with pros and cons of doing the play or musical you have researched as a school production. Answer these questions about the play or musical:* Is it easy / difficult to stage? Is there a suitable number of acting roles? Is it suitable for a school play audience?

READING

3 *Me, My Selfie & I* by Jonathan Dorf → 131/2; S2

Read the following scene from Me, My Selfie & I, *a one-act dramedy by Jonathan Dorf. Use a dictionary for help. What is it about?*

VIP File

Jonathan Dorf is a US playwright and screenwriter[1]. His plays have been produced all over the world. He has written a number of plays for young adults. One of them is *Me, My Selfie & I*, a series of short scenes that deal with the way we live in a world of social media. In this play, the audience gets to know a group of teens who struggle with finding a balance between recording their lives for social media and actually living them.

The Man in the Mirror

(MIRROR BOY, a teen boy in a muscle tee and with a cell phone in his hand, poses in front of the BOY'S MIRROR, dressed identically and mirroring him completely throughout the scene. Mirror Boy does a "double bicep" pose.)

MIRROR BOY: Do you think girls are gonna go for this?
BOY'S MIRROR: I'm just the mirror.
MIRROR BOY: I know, but you've seen me for the last few months.
BOY'S MIRROR: Seen you for way longer than that.
MIRROR BOY: You know what I mean. Since I've been bodybuilding.
BOY'S MIRROR: Is that what you call it?
MIRROR BOY: Fine. Working out.
BOY'S MIRROR: OK – that's fair.
MIRROR BOY: *(Doing a "most muscular" pose:)* So?
BOY'S MIRROR: That looks painful.
MIRROR BOY: It is. And hard to take a picture while you're doing it.
BOY'S MIRROR: Hmm …
(Mirror Boy releases the pose.)
MIRROR BOY: *(Pulling up his shirt to show off his abs:)* Or what about this?
BOY'S MIRROR: Better than it was.
MIRROR BOY: Better than it was. *(Beat.)* But not good?
BOY'S MIRROR: If you say so.
MIRROR BOY: What do *you* say?
BOY'S MIRROR: If you think about it, I say what you say.
MIRROR BOY: So if I say which pic should I post–
BOY'S MIRROR: Which pic do you want to post?
MIRROR BOY: And should I do a shirtless …?
BOY'S MIRROR: Do you want to?
MIRROR BOY: This isn't helpful.
BOY'S MIRROR: Who are you taking pictures for?
(Beat.)
MIRROR BOY: I don't know.
BOY'S MIRROR: Maybe if you answer that, you'll know how to answer the other ones.

Reading skills

A **dramedy** is a play that is supposed to be both funny and serious. It's a mixture between a drama and a comedy. Do you know any plays (or series and films) that fall into that category? What other genres do you know of? What are their characteristics?

1 screenwriter ['skri:nraɪtə] sb who writes scripts for films

READING

4 Understanding and analysing a scene → SB 136/3; S4, S5, S8

a) *Describe your first reaction. Use your exercise book.*

b) *Tick ✔ the correct answer.*

1. What is the main theme of the scene?
   - a) ☐ teenagers and the image they have of themselves
   - b) ☐ bodybuilding and working out
   - c) ☐ posting photos on social media
2. What is the boy most concerned about?
   - a) ☐ taking a really good photo of himself
   - b) ☐ how others will see him
   - c) ☐ the pros and cons of bodybuilding
3. How is the situation unusual or unexpected?
   - a) ☐ The boy's reflection[1] is an independent character.
   - b) ☐ The boy's reflection says things that many people prefer not to think about.
   - c) ☐ The boy and his reflection have different physical images.
4. Describe the conflict between the characters (the boy and his reflection).
   - a) ☐ The reflection is rude to the boy.
   - b) ☐ The reflection keeps telling the boy what to do.
   - c) ☐ The reflection avoids answering the boy's questions.
5. Describe the register used by the characters.
   - a) ☐ neutral
   - b) ☐ quite informal
   - c) ☐ extremely informal
6. Choose the best interpretation of the message of the dénouement.
   - a) ☐ The boy realises that he should be less concerned about his appearance.
   - b) ☐ Social media makes people worry too much about their appearance.
   - c) ☐ The scene represents the boy starting to realise his motivations.

c) *Identify the tone used by each character (e.g. ironic, sarcastic, emotional, confused, angry, nervous, bored …). Where **more than one** answer is possible, suggest the different possibilities.*

SPEAKING

5 Act out the scene → SB 136/4

a) *Prepare and practise the scene. Decide who will play which character. Think about how to use your voice:*

- Mark stresses, pauses and rising / falling intonation in the playscript on p. 62.
- Play with different tones: Use your ideas from ex. 4c). Try different voice levels and speeds of delivery.

b) *Record two or more different versions with different emotions, voice levels etc. and choose the best one. Analyse why it is the best.*

1 reflection [rɪˈflekʃn] *here:* an image in a mirror

WRITING

6 Write a scene → SB 137/1; S5, S8

Write a new scene in which a character and their reflection have a conversation. Use an idea from these photos or your own ideas. The scene can be humorous, serious or fantasy. Follow the steps on pp. 137–138 in your book. These extra ideas may be useful:

- Think about conflict between the characters. What do they disagree on? How does their conversation develop?
- Try to end with a really strong final line. Perhaps write this line first, and write the rest of the scene to fit.

A

B

C

D

E

F

G

On these pages you are going to practise doing the types of tasks you will do in the ZP10 (*Zentrale Prüfung Klasse 10, Nordrhein-Westfalen*). You are also going to get some useful tips on how to deal with the tasks successfully.

1 Reading: Historic lands

Canadian government signs historic settlement[1] with Siksika First Nation

$1.3 billion payment will "right a wrong from the past," says Prime Minister Trudeau

As Canadian readers will already know, Canada continues to deal with its colonial past by settling 'land claims'. These claims involve First Nations peoples taking back control of their historic lands or, where this is no longer possible, being paid compensation for land that was illegally taken from them. So far, Canada has found a solution for nearly 600 of these claims by reaching settlements with First Nations across the country.

The latest land claim settlement is also one of the largest ever agreed in Canada. Today Prime Minister Justin Trudeau, Chief Ouray Crowfoot of Siksika Nation and other Siksika council and community members met on Siksika territory near Calgary, Alberta for a ceremony to announce the signing of the $1.3 billion settlement.

In 1877, Government of Canada signed a treaty with Siksika Nation to guarantee them ownership of their historic lands. However, in later years the government broke the treaty and almost half of this land - including some of the Siksika's best agricultural land - was taken to be sold to settlers or used for other purposes such as mining and building rail tracks. The first Siksika Nation land claim was made in 1960, but it has taken until now to finally solve the issue.

Crowfoot said, "Canada is not giving $1.3 billion to Siksika. Canada is righting a wrong committed over a century ago when Canada illegally took 115,000 acres of lands provided to Siksika along with other illegal acts." He went on to say, "Canada needs to stop using the word 'reconciliation[2]'. You will never reconcile, you will never make it whole," but said that the settlement will make a positive difference to his people's lives and will provide new opportunities for them. He added, "I do see the tide turning for Siksika. I see us becoming a thriving[3] nation."

Trudeau described the settlement as "an opportunity to look forward as we build a better future together - one that is based on nation-to-nation dialogue, partnership, and respect." Also at the ceremony was Marc Miller, minister of Crown-Indigenous relations. He said, "Today's celebrations mark a turning point in our relationship with Siksika Nation, as we continue to move forward to strengthen our relationship and support Siksika's vision of a better future for their people."

Siksika's website reports that each member of the Siksika Nation (which has around 8,000 members) will receive $20,000 as part of the settlement. Desmond Pelly, a young member of the Siksika Nation, commented, "You know it can be very beneficial for a lot of people, you know it can mean getting a new vehicle, being able to go to college, getting a better experience, getting a better chance at life. It's a light at the end of a dark tunnel for a lot of people that are struggling with poverty."

Although the Siksika settlement is one of the largest yet made, it is very much not the end of Canada's land claim story. Land claim negotiations[4] between the government and several other First Nations are still going on. There has been much positive development, but the government has been criticised for the way in which it assesses[5] claims and for its slowness in dealing with them.

1 settlement ['setlmənt] *here:* payment or other action to end a dispute ○ **2** reconciliation [ˌreknˌsɪli'eɪʃn] ending of conflict between former enemies ○ **3** to thrive ['θraɪv] to be healthy and / or successful ○ **4** negotiation [nɪˌgəʊʃɪ'eɪʃn] formal discussion in order to find a suitable compromise ○ **5** to assess [ə'ses] to judge the quality of sb / sth

You are doing a school project about Canada. During research you found the article above about a recent event. Tick ✔ the correct box and give one piece of evidence by quoting short passages from the text.

1. Land claims pay back First Nations for …
   a) ☐ damage to their land.
   b) ☐ stolen territory.
   c) ☐ all past wrongs.

   ____

   ____

2. The signing ceremony was attended by representatives of the government and …
   a) ☐ the Calgary council.
   b) ☐ the Siksika Nation.
   c) ☐ several First Nations.

   ____

   ____

3. The land claim exists because Canada …
   a) ☐ ignored a contract.
   b) ☐ took all Siksika territory.
   c) ☐ changed Siksika territory to farmland.

   ____

   ____

4. Crowfoot feels that to describe this situation, the word 'reconciliation' is not …
   a) ☐ strong enough.
   b) ☐ the only option.
   c) ☐ correct.

   ____

   ____

5. Crowfoot believes the Siksika people have …
   a) ☐ a positive future.
   b) ☐ more claims to make.
   c) ☐ new friends in the government.

   ____

   ____

6. Some people feel that land claims by other First Nations are …
   a) ☐ not likely to be settled.
   b) ☐ too small.
   c) ☐ not moving quickly enough.

   ____

   ____

7. Match the people with the descriptions. There is one more description than you need.

   1. Crowfoot
   2. Justin Trudeau
   3. Marc Miller
   4. Desmond Pelly

   a) talks about future communication between the two sides
   b) gives hope to other First Nations with land claims
   c) gives examples of how the compensation will be used
   d) corrects a false idea about the settlement
   e) sees the ceremony as the start of a new era

   1. _____ 2. _____

   3. _____ 4. _____

Tip

Check for words which are repeated from the text or are synonyms for words in the text, but may lead you to choosing the wrong answer. Look at the information which comes before and after that point in the text.

2 Vocabulary: First Nations peoples and communities

Read about the historical context and meaning of terms that are now used in preference to 'Indian'. Fill in suitable words or tick ✔ the correct box. Give only one solution.

1. The USA and Canada were both British ______________________.
   a) ☐ empires b) ☐ colonies c) ☐ invasions d) ☐ states
2. From the late 17th century, large numbers of people from Europe came to North America as ______________________ and established new homes there.
3. This was a disaster for the ______________________ population.
4. Many died from new (to them) ______________________ that had been brought by the colonists.
5. The survivors were forced to leave some or all of their homelands and live in areas called ______________________ (USA) or reserves (Canada). (Today, though, the majority of Native American / First Nations people live in urban areas.)
   a) ☐ reservations b) ☐ conserves c) ☐ retreats d) ☐ preserves
6. The ______________________ of these people are correctly described as Native Americans in the USA.
   a) ☐ elders b) ☐ descendants c) ☐ allies d) ☐ representatives
7. In Canada, they are ______________________ to as Inuit, Métis or members of the First Nations, depending on their ethnic origins.
8. In both countries, the colonial-______________________ term 'Indian' is still used too.
   a) ☐ time b) ☐ era c) ☐ state d) ☐ moment
9. However, this term is increasingly considered to be ______________________.
10. More than ever before, there is a wish to celebrate Native American, First Nation, Métis and Inuit cultural ______________________.
11. Some Native American / First Nations peoples are spread across the United States-Canada ______________________.
12. An example are the Anishinaabe peoples, a group of culturally-related ______________________ which originated in the Great Lakes area of the USA / Canada.
    a) ☐ gatherings c) ☐ communes
    b) ☐ communities d) ☐ reserves

Tip

Filling gaps
When you are asked to fill a gap yourself, more than one answer may be correct so there is no pressure to find the 'perfect' word. It's important that the text makes sense with your answer and that you use the correct form of the word.

3 Writing: Firekeeper's Daughter

Firekeeper's Daughter *by Angeline Boulley is a novel for young adults. It follows eighteen-year-old Daunis, a girl of mixed Native American and European heritage. GrandMary is Daunis's name for her white grandmother, whom she is visiting in the old people's home.*

GrandMary blinks and her eyes brighten. Just like that, her focus sharpens, and she is once again a mighty force of nature, the Fontaine matriarch.

"GrandMary," I say quickly. "I'm deferring[1] my admission to U of M[2] and registering for classes at Lake State. Just for freshman year." I hold my breath, anticipating her disappointment in my deviation from the Plan: Daunis Lorenza Fontaine, MD[3].

At first, I went along with it, hoping to make her proud. I pretended so well, and for so long, that her plan became my plan. Our plan. I loved that plan. But that was in the Before.

GrandMary fixes me with a gaze as tender as my mother's kisses. Something passes between my grandmother and me. She understands why I had to alter our plan.

My nose tingles with pre-cry pinpricks from relief, sadness, or both. Maybe there's a word in Anishinaabemowin[4] for when you find solid footing in the rubble after a tragedy.

Mom rushes around the bed, pulling me into an embrace that whooshes the air from my lungs. Her joyful sobs vibrate through me. I made my mother happy. I knew I would, but I didn't expect to feel such relief myself. She's been pushing for me not to go away to college. Mom pleaded with me to fill out the Lake State admissions form back in January as a birthday gift to her. I agreed, thinking there was no way anything would come to pass. Turns out, there was a way.

A bird thuds against the window. I only get three steps toward the window when the bird rises, fluttering to regain equilibrium before resuming its journey.

Gramma Pearl – my Anishinaabe nokomis[5] on my Firekeeper side – considered a bird flying into a window a bad sign. She would rush outside, one leathered brown hand at her mouth, muttering "uh- uh-oh" at its crooked neck before calling her sisters to figure out which tragedy was just around the corner.

But GrandMary would say it was random and unfortunate. Nothing more than an unintended consequence of a clean window. *Indian superstitions are not facts, Daunis.*

My Zhaaganaash[6] and Anishinaabe grandmothers could not have been more different. One viewed the world as its surface, while the other saw connections and teachings that run deeper than our known world. Their push and pull on me has been a tug-of-war my entire life.

When I was seven, I spent a weekend at Gramma Pearl's house on Sugar Island. I woke up crying with an earache, but the ferry to the mainland had shut down for the night. She had me pee in a cup, and poured it into my ear as I rested my head in her lap. Back home for Sunday dinner at GrandMary and Grandpa Lorenzo's, I excitedly shared how smart my other grandmother was. *Gramma Pearl fixed my earache with my pee!* GrandMary recoiled and, a heartbeat later, glared at my mother as if this was her fault. Something split inside me when I saw my mother's embarrassment. I learned there were times when I was expected to be a Fontaine and other times when it was safe to be a Firekeeper.

A week ago, I woke up during one of Mom's cleaning frenzies.

I've lost so much, David. And now her. When Daunis leaves, j'disparaîtrai.

She used the French word for "disappear." To fade or pass away.

Gramma Pearl always told me, *Bad things happen in threes.*

Uncle David died in April. GrandMary had a stroke in June. If I stay home, I can stop the third bad thing from happening. Even if it means waiting a little longer to follow the Plan.

From: Angeline Boulley, *Firekeeper's Daughter*, 2021 (abridged)

1 to defer [dɪˈfɜː] to stop sth and continue at a later time ◯ **2** U of M stands for 'University of Michigan' ◯ **3** MD stands for 'medical doctor' ◯ **4** Anishinaabemowin an Indigenous language of North America ◯ **5** nokomis 'my grandmother' in Anishinaabemowin ◯ **6** Zhaaganaash 'English / British / white person' in Anishinaabemowin

Read the tasks carefully. Make sure to write about all the aspects presented in each task.

a) ***Describe*** *the situation that Daunis is in and how she deals with it.*

b) ***Analyse*** *conflicts in Daunis's life plans and in her family situation. In doing so, look at the way that aspects of Native American / First Nations and non-Native American / non-First Nations culture are described.*

c) *Here you can choose between three different options. Do only* ***one*** *of them.*

Tip

Expanding your vocabulary will generally make you more confident in using the English language. Starting from now, what can you personally do to increase the number of words you know? Reviewing relevant grammar topics (like tenses, relative clauses, word order …) is also a good way to prepare for writing tasks.

Option 1:

Comment on the title of the novel *Firekeeper's Daughter*. Include the following aspects:
- What do you think 'firekeeper' may mean, and what does the title suggest about the themes of the book?
- Is it a good title for the book? Why? Why not?
- Would you like to read the book? Why? Why not?

Or

Option 2:

Write an email from Daunis to a close friend who is not from a Native American / First Nations background.
Include the following aspects:
- how and why you have changed your future plans,
- how you feel about this,
- why it may be difficult for other people to understand your decision.

Start:
Hi!
Big news – I've changed my plans.

Or

Option 3:

Write a continuation of the story. Daunis describes her hopes for her future life.
Include the following aspects:
- her hopes for her future education and work,
- her wishes to stay connected with both sides of her family and her Native American / First Nations culture,
- her thoughts about things that may go wrong.

Start:
My thoughts keep turning to my future. I want to … / I don't want to …

Bildquellennachweis:
U1.1 Unsplash, Montréal, QC (Daniel Novykov); **U1.2** plainpicture GmbH & Co. KG RF, Hamburg (DEEPOL); **4.1** ShutterStock.com RF, New York (Alex from the Rock); **5.1** Rau, Katja, Berglen; **6.1** Alamy stock photo, Abingdon (ton koene); **7.1** ShutterStock.com RF, New York (arindambanerjee); **8.1** ShutterStock.com RF, New York (guruXOX); **9.1** ShutterStock.com RF, New York (Renee Clancy); **10.1** ShutterStock.com RF, New York (Atakan Yildiz); **11.1** CartoonStock Ltd, Bath (Crowden Satz); **11.2** CartoonStock Ltd, Bath (Fran); **12.1** Cover aus der Reihe Klett English Readers: Burning Sunlight von Anthea Simmons; Klett English Editions, ISBN 978-3-12-542652-8, © Ernst Klett Sprachen GmbH, Stuttgart 2021; **13.1** ShutterStock.com RF, New York (KK_face); **17.1** ShutterStock.com RF, New York (Electric Egg); **18.1** ShutterStock.com RF, New York (ihsan kamal); **19.1** ShutterStock.com RF, New York (Gorodenkoff); **19.2** ShutterStock.com RF, New York (Kaspars Grinvalds); **19.3** ShutterStock.com RF, New York (Bilderstoeckchen); **19.4** ShutterStock.com RF, New York (Sean Locke Photography); **19.5** ShutterStock.com RF, New York (on_france); **19.6** ShutterStock.com RF, New York (Afanasieva); **19.7** ShutterStock.com RF, New York (Kriang kan); **20.1** ShutterStock.com RF, New York (Chaay_Tee); **20.2** CartoonStock Ltd, Bath (Dave Carpenter); **21.1** ShutterStock.com RF, New York (Olga Gladkikkh); **21.2** ShutterStock.com RF, New York (DavideAngelini); **22.1** Getty Images Plus, München (Halfpoint Images); **23.1** ShutterStock.com RF, New York (Eireen.zn); **25.1** ShutterStock.com RF, New York (Lia_Russy); **27.1** ShutterStock.com RF, New York (Perfect Wave); **29.1** ShutterStock.com RF, New York (dotshock); **29.2** ShutterStock.com RF, New York (oneinchpunch); **29.3** ShutterStock.com RF, New York (KarlosWest); **29.4** ShutterStock.com RF, New York (Roberto Sorin); **30.1** ShutterStock.com RF, New York (Gorodenkoff); **31.1** ShutterStock.com RF, New York (MicroOne); **33.2** ShutterStock.com RF, New York (wavebreakmedia); **34.1** ShutterStock.com RF, New York (Photographee.eu); **36.1** ShutterStock.com RF, New York (charactervectorart); **37.1** ShutterStock.com RF, New York (Supamotionstock.com); **37.2** ShutterStock.com RF, New York (My Agency); **37.3** ShutterStock.com RF, New York (Gorodenkoff); **38.1** ShutterStock.com RF, New York (Rawpixel.com); **41.1** ShutterStock.com RF, New York (oliveromg); **46.1** stock.adobe.com, Dublin (vospalej); **46.2** ShutterStock.com RF, New York (Jody Ann); **46.3** ShutterStock.com RF, New York (Maani Collection); **46.4** ShutterStock.com RF, New York (Lucky Business); **46.5** ShutterStock.com RF, New York (David Tadevosian); **46.6** ShutterStock.com RF, New York (saiko3p); **48.1** ShutterStock.com RF, New York (Ammit Jack); **50.1** Mauritius RF, Mittenwald (Alamy/Reeldeal Images); **50.2** ShutterStock.com RF, New York (Monkey Business Images); **51.1** stock.adobe.com, Dublin (Stockwerk-Fotodesign); **52.1** Mauritius Images, Mittenwald (Alamy Stock Photos); **53.1** ShutterStock.com RF, New York (Alexey Seafarer); **53.2** ShutterStock.com RF, New York (Sergei Bachlakov); **53.3** Mauritius Images, Mittenwald (Alamy Stock Photos); **53.4** Mauritius Images, Mittenwald (Alamy Stock Photos); **53.5** ShutterStock.com RF, New York (pr2is); **53.6** ShutterStock.com RF, New York (Gorloff-KV); **54.1** CartoonStock Ltd, Bath (Fakes, Nate); **55.1** Illustrations from THE OUTSIDE CIRCLE reproduced with permission from House of Anansi Press, Toronto. Text copyright © 2015 by Patti LaBoucane-Benson, illustrations copyright © Native Counselling Services of Alberta. www.houseofanansi.com; **55.2** Illustrations from THE OUTSIDE CIRCLE reproduced with permission from House of Anansi Press, Toronto. Text copyright © 2015 by Patti LaBoucane-Benson, illustrations copyright © Native Counselling Services of Alberta. www.houseofanansi.com; **56.1** Illustrations from THE OUTSIDE CIRCLE reproduced with permission from House of Anansi Press, Toronto. Text copyright © 2015 by Patti LaBoucane-Benson, illustrations copyright © Native Counselling Services of Alberta. www.houseofanansi.com; **57.1** Illustrations from THE OUTSIDE CIRCLE reproduced with permission from House of Anansi Press, Toronto. Text copyright © 2015 by Patti LaBoucane-Benson, illustrations copyright © Native Counselling Services of Alberta. www.houseofanansi.com; **60.1** ShutterStock.com RF, New York (Lina Chekhovich); **61.1** Mauritius Images, Mittenwald (Randy Duchaine/Alamy Stock Photo); **62.1** Jonathan Dorf (Chad Runyon); **62.2** ShutterStock.com RF, New York (Golubovy); **64.1** ShutterStock.com RF, New York (Volodymyr Burdiak); **64.2** ShutterStock.com RF, New York (ME Image); **64.3** ShutterStock.com RF, New York (Dmytro Zinkevych); **64.4** ShutterStock.com RF, New York (Yiistocking); **64.5** ShutterStock.com RF, New York (Hitdelight); **64.6** ShutterStock.com RF, New York (Yuganov Konstantin); **64.7** ShutterStock.com RF, New York (serg_dibrova); **69.1** ShutterStock.com RF, New York (zause01)

Textquellennachweis:
12–14 From: Burning Sunlight ©2021 Anthea Simmons; Zur besseren altersgemäßen Verständlichkeit wurde der Originaltext verändert, ohne den Inhalt und/oder Sinn zu verändern.; **21** © Copyright Sideqik 2022; **23** Adapted from: Elizabeth Joy, 2021 https://www.consciouslifeandstyle.com; Zur besseren altersgemäßen Verständlichkeit wurde der Originaltext verändert, ohne den Inhalt und/oder Sinn zu verändern.; **30** ZEIT ONLINE, Fabian Held, 4. März 2021; **32–34** Adpated from: One of Us Is Lying © 2017 Karen M. McManus; Zur besseren altersgemäßen Verständlichkeit wurde der Originaltext verändert, ohne den Inhalt und/oder Sinn zu verändern.; **44–45** From: Click'd ©2019 Tamara Ireland Stone; Zur besseren altersgemäßen Verständlichkeit wurde der Originaltext verändert, ohne den Inhalt und/oder Sinn zu verändern.; **55–57** From: The Outside Circle ©2015 Patti LaBoucane-Benson; **62** The Man in the Mirror from: Me, My Selfie & I, Jonathan Dorf, 2017, Youthplays.com; **65.1–8** Justin Trudeau, quoted in PM signs historic land claim settlement with Siksika First Nation, 02.06.2022, www.cbc.ca; Chief Ouray Crowfoot of Siksika Nation, quoted in PM signs historic land claim settlement with Siksika First Nation, 02.06.2022, www.cbc.ca; Chief Ouray Crowfoot of Siksika Nation, quoted in PM signs historic land claim settlement with Siksika First Nation, 02.06.2022, www.cbc.ca; Chief Ouray Crowfoot of Siksika Nation, quoted in Major historical claim settlement with Siksika Nation, 02.06.2022, https://siksikanation.com; Justin Trudeau, quoted in Major historical claim settlement with Siksika Nation, 02.06.2022, https://siksikanation.com; Marc Miller, quoted in Major historical claim settlement with Siksika Nation, 02.06.2022, https://siksikanation.com; Desmond Pelly quoted in Prime Minister signs historic land claim settlement with Siksika First Nation. 03.06.2022, https://calgary.ctvnews.ca/; **68** From: Firekeeper's daughter ©2022 Angeline Boulley; Zur besseren altersgemäßen Verständlichkeit wurde der Originaltext verändert, ohne den Inhalt und/oder Sinn zu verändern.